Christmas '79

Bill

Hopes hereing ---er
here's hoping you
will enjoy this
every minute or
two when you
get a chance!
Laughingly loving
(or should that be
lovingly laughing?)
Mom

PRIZE BLOOPERS

BOOKS
BY KERMIT SCHAFER

Best of Bloopers
All-Time Great Bloopers
Super Duper Bloopers
Blunderful World of Bloopers
Typo-Bloopers
CB Citizen's Bloopers
Blooper Tube

RECORD ALBUMS

Pardon My Blooper Vol. 1-2

Pardon My Blooper Vol. 3-4

Pardon My Blooper Vol. 5-6

Blunderful World of Bloopers
2-record set

All-Time Great Bloopers
6-volume set

Blooper Awards

Sports Bloopers

PRIZE BLOOPERS

UNBLEEPED!

Radio and TV's Most Hilarious Boners
Collected by Radio-TV Producer
KERMIT SCHAFER
AUTHOR OF BEST SELLING BLOOPER BOOKS

AVENEL BOOKS • NEW YORK

Copyright ©MCMLXXIX by Blooper Enterprises, Inc., a division of Kermit
Schafer Productions
All rights reserved.
This edition is published by Avenel Books, distributed by Crown Publishers, Inc.
a b c d e f g h
AVENEL 1979 PRINTING
Manufactured in the United States of America

Library of Congress Cataloging in Publication Data

Schafer, Kermit, 1914-1979
    Prize bloopers.

    1. Broadcasting—United States—Anecdotes,
facetiae, satire.   I. Title.
PN1990.87.S34   791.44′02′907   78-31539
ISBN 0-517-27832-4

DEDICATION

This book is dedicated as a sympathetic tribute to members of the broadcasting industry who have been the victims of Bloopers, in the hope that it offers consolation and proof of the fact that they are not alone.

To err is human,
To forgive, divine.
Alexander Pope

To forgive is human,
To err, divine.
Kermit Schafer

PRIZE BLOOPERS

Nuts to You

Disc jockey Johnny Cee walked into the radio booth while another DJ was on the air. Johnny was scratching himself in a rather inappropriate place when the other DJ asked him what he was doing. Johnny said, "I'm scratching my nuts." When he noticed that the mike was open, he quickly added, ". . . and bolts. Beep, beep. I'm a robot!"

Now You See It ... Now You Don't

SPORTSCASTER: "Bob Griese, the Miami Dolphin quarterback, has blurred vision and will not see action for the rest of the game."

Judy! Judy!

Heard on "Family Feud" on ABC-TV: "Here with me are my son Tom, my son Tim, and my son Judy."

You Bet Your Ass!

On "Saturday Night Live" on NBC-TV after a skit bombed, comedian Jack Burns introduced a film in this fashion: "And now, here is this week's film by Gary Weiss. It's a satire of *Rocky*, and who knows, maybe it'll save my ass!"

Truth in Advertising

ANNOUNCER: "Our departing contestants on 'Wheel of Fortune' will receive a $25 gift certificate good at any Dairy Queen, home of the scrumptious, dillishit, I mean, delicious burger."

Hooked!

On "Liar's Club" Dody Goodman had a wooden object she called a "rug hooker." After demonstrating it, she blooped, "In some communities in India, they'll have as many as 25 hookers sitting around." The emcee promptly took the object away from her.

Wall Banger

On "The Price Is Right" Bob Barker asked "Okay, Johnny, what's our next item going up for bid on 'The Price Is Right'?" Johnny Olsen replied, "A beautiful wall cock . . . clock!"

A Sad Tale

COMMERCIAL: "For all your nudes . . . er, needs, remember to visit Mrs. Wooler's Tail Stop . . . TAILOR SHOP!"

Don't Miss It if You Can

During a television interview, actress Susan Oliver blooped, "I wouldn't miss this for all the leis in Hawaii."

A Big Song

On "The Tonight Show" on NBC-TV, Johnny Carson, discussing the fact that the movie *King Kong* didn't win any Academy Awards other than for sound effects, blooped, "I understand that *King Song* . . . (AUDIENCE LAUGHTER) . . . *Sing Song* . . . *King Kong!!*"

Exciting Tour

NEWSCASTER: "South Moluccan tourists were holding 105 children at gunpoint ... I mean, TERRORISTS!"

Spreading the Rumors

COMMENTATOR: "At Annapolis rumors continued that officials decided to spread the women through the 36 companies of midshipmen."

Game Called

DJ Donnie McCrary was doing a radio broadcast of a baseball game for KUOA, Salome Springs, Arkansas. The game went into extra innings, and he began to tire. During a rally the fans began to clap, and the DJ was heard to say, "The clouds are crapping."

An Elephant Never Forgets

During a broadcast on WLVT in Bethlehem, Pennsylvania, in which high school students compete for scholarships, the emcee asked, "What information does the atomic number of an elephant, uh, elephant, uh, what information does the atomic number of an element convey?"

Take It Off!

On WYDD-FM radio a sportscaster announced, "Mr. Bailey will strip down from his position as head basketball coach ... STEP DOWN!!"

Super Imposition

On Channel 5 in St. Louis it was reported that a lady in Illinois had developed a product for plants made of pig manure that was deodorized. She said that it was as good as cow manure. The reporter was interviewing her when her name and the name of the product appeared at the bottom of the screen:

Mary Kaye Harmon
Pig Poo Pusher

Flies in the Ointment

During "Password" Allen Ludden was doing a commercial for Del Monte's catsup when he said, "One bottle will cover hundreds of French flies."

If You Can't Beat 'Em ... Eat 'Em!

On a television quiz show the question was asked, "For $20 what is the only part of the human body that is edible?" (AUDIENCE HYSTERIA)

Obscene Phone Call

News programs originating from overseas depend on the telephone companies to furnish their facilities for transmissions from abroad with the result that all of the networks have to wait their turn for the use of these facilities.

NEWS COMMENTATOR: "NBC Moscow standing by. (OFF MIKE) What makes me mad, you know, what they say at the other end. They tell New York that the Moscow correspondent isn't in ... that he doesn't accept the call. I've been here for three hours. You beat your brains, you work like hell, fight the fuckin' censors ... Everything is normal ... like a bucket of shit is normal."

No Comment

A flustered sports announcer described the following during a football game: "And there goes a whopping 63-yard CUNT ... I mean, kick ... PUNT!!!!"

Cut Throat

A local radio announcer on a Eugene, Oregon, radio station was discussing Linda Lovelace of *Deep Throat* fame. His final comment was, ... "Would you believe this? They want us to believe it. Linda Lovelace is starring in a new movie, *Linda Lovelace for President*. ... Aw, c'mon. I can't swallow that!"

The College of Your Choice

When former President Ford was visiting Ames, Iowa, the home of Iowa State University, his speech began with, "I am glad to be at Ohio State University."

Off the Record

A novice disc jockey was working at a radio station as a sub-
stitute. Coming out of the network news, he would bring the
sound up on a record and then fade it under a commercial,
which was recorded on a cartridge. He was desperately trying to
get the commercial to play. After the cartridge failed to work, the
record turntable broke down. In frustration he exclaimed,
"Doesn't any of these pig-fucking sonofabitches work?" It was the
last time he substituted on that station.

To Each His Own

NBC's Critic-at-Large, Leon Pearson, advised that he would now
review the new feature which had opened the night before:
"Desire Under the Arms . . . that should be *ELMS!"*

A Scientific Period

On "The Tonight Show," guest host John Denver was discussing the arrival of the Comet Kohoutek and said to his guest, "We will be watching for Comet Kotex next month."

Bottoms Up

"The Great American Birthday Celebration" was hosted by Ed McMahon, and many in the TV audience spotted this Blooper. During the second hour of the program, the First Continental Navy Jack was pictured with WHITE stripes at the top and the bottom.

Jiminy Cricket

A day of whistle-stopping across mid-America apparently got to Walter Mondale. After making essentially the same speech all day, the Democratic Vice Presidential candidate slipped during his appearance in Fort Wayne, Indiana, and referred to Jimmy Carter as "Jimmy Ford." He caught himself and said, "Forgive me, Jimmy."

All Shook Up

Irrepressible Tom Snyder zinged his network on his "Tomorrow Show" when he noted that the previous "Today Show" on NBC-TV "did an interview with a man who says there's an earthquake imminent in California, and people ought to be prepared." Then noted Snyder, "The network in its wisdom did a station break that said: 'See *Earthquake,* the big event on NBC this fall.' We've got some brains here, I'll tell you."

Fault

Tom Seaver's stint as sportscaster was not without its flubs. He referred to tennis star Evonne Goolagong as Evonne Googalong.

Laugh, Clown, Laugh

During an audience warm-up, which ran over the allotted time, the nationwide audience heard Al Jolson tell his studio audience, ". . . and if you don't laugh, you can get the hell out of here!"

H-E-R-E's John!

On "The Tonight Show" when Johnny Carson was cutting to a commercial, he said to a guest off camera, "All commercials are used for is to give people a chance to go to the john!"

No News Is Good News

John Shubeck of Channel 4 did a one-minute news update and stated: "This afternoon, E. Howard Cunt . . . uh . . . E. Howard Hunt held a news conference."

Boob Tube

A novice female disc jockey on KWYD, Fountain, Colorado, was doing a late night radio show to gain experience. The engineer came into the studio. She did not realize that her mike was open. The audience heard her say, "Quit that! I'm not used to having my boobs played with on the air!"

Cockeyed

A new announcer was asked to read the news. It was during Archibald Cox's reign as Watergate prosecutor. What the audience heard was, "This is KWRO News. Special Watergate prosecutor Archibald's Cock, uh ... Archiball's Cock ... uh, Archibald's Cock ..." Then dead silence as the engineer desperately cued a commerical minutes ahead of schedule.

Fall On Your As-pen

SKI REPORT: "And now the Ski Report from Aspen where the skis are scattered ... SKIES."

Truth Is Stranger Than Fiction

On "To Tell the Truth" a gentleman claiming to be a biologist was asked if it were true that large numbers of fish were to be found around the offshore oil rigs and if so, why? The gentleman said that it was true and the reason for their being there was because of the many orgasms . . . which he quickly changed to organisms.

Get Up and Go

On KIKM Radio, Sherman, Texas, a tired-sounding Santa Claus was attempting a few weak ho hos while imploring people to see about his sponsor's Christmas sale. One unfortunate DJ remarked on an open mike that "Santa needs a laxative or a new ho hoer!"

Snow Bird

Having worked with Allen Funt as producer of his "Candid Mike" record album, I can tell you that the following, although it might sound like it, is definitely not a "Candid Camera" put on.

SKI REPORTER: "The weather was clear. The people gave quite an ovation to Buddy Werner when he came in on his last effort to unseat the champion."

PRODUCER: "Where's my close? Where the hell is my close? Will you identify yourself and say, 'Now back to Monitor in Radio Central.' "

SKI REPORTER: "This is Kit Carson White, the ski reporter from San Francisco. I'd like to return you back to Monitor in San Francisco."

PRODUCER: "Look, Kit, you say your name is Kit Carson

White? Would you please say, 'This is Kit Carson White in Squaw Valley. Now back to Monitor in Radio Central.' "

SKI REPORTER: "This is Kit Carson White from Squaw Valley. Now back to Radio Monitor in Radio Central."

PRODUCER: "Let's try it again. It's Monitor in Radio Central."

SKI REPORTER: "In Radio Central. All right. This is Kit Carson White in Squaw Valley, and now back to Radio Monitor in Central."

PRODUCER: (BREAKING UP) "Kit, let's try it slow this time. It's Monitor in Radio Central."

SKI REPORTER: "Okay, Let me write it down . . . okay, Monitor in Radio Central. All right. This is Kit Carson White from Squaw Valley. And now back to Radio Monitor in Central!"

The Cat's Meow

Station WDHO, Channel 24, Toledo, Ohio,was showing a commercial about Pampers diapers. The video was about the diaper, but the audio was about cat food. It went on to say as the woman was holding up the diaper, "Look, no mess, no smell."

That's No Lady ... That's My Wife

A reporter for the public radio network carrying the activities of the inaugural ceremonies was on the platform interviewing dignitaries and said, "I'm here interviewing Senator and Mrs. John Danforth." Danforth broke in and said, "This is Senator (Thomas F.) Eagleton. My wife isn't here." Eagleton was bundled in a black topcoat and black and gray shawl wrapped around his head in the fashion of a woman's scarf.

Right On

WTOP newsman Gordon Peterson announced, "Today a baby elephant was born ... (PAUSING A SECOND) ... I guess all elephants born are babies."

A Mart-yr

Bob Fuller of KLYB, Bakersfield, California, fluffed this commercial: "Free groceries will be given away at the grand opening of the new Thrifty Fart Store in Oildale."

Pea-nuts

"Tomorrow Show's" Tom Snyder was having his usual impromptu monologue at the beginning of his show when he said, "President Carter and his balls will be in Washington, D.C., tonight for the inauguration parties." (CREW AND CAMERAMEN BURST OUT LAUGHING.) Snyder blushed and rephrased himself saying, "C'mon, you guys, I meant his inaugural balls."

Watch Your Step!

ANNOUNCER: "So for great savings on shoes during our New Year's sale, stop at any of our Shoe Shitty stores closest to you."

Three's a Crowd

Ted Henry of WEWS, Cleveland, Ohio, read this news item about a robbery: "A clothing store today was held up by three armed men."

Nutty Tip

An "ABC News" daily consumer tip was given thus: "In between use, you should freeze your nuts to keep them fresh."

By George

McLean Stevenson was substituting on "The Tonight Show." His first guest was George Blanda, and after asking a few questions, they broke for a commercial. Stevenson, not realizing the mike was open, said, "Jesus Christ, I don't know what to ask him ... what kind of questions do you ask a guy who's been playing football for 24 years?"

Half Fast

Heard on KEVY radio, Provo, Utah: An announcer was doing a remote broadcast, and the turntable had been set up in rather cold weather. It started slowly and just couldn't build up speed. As the record was sounding horrible, the DJ felt that he had to do something, so he said, "Our chipmunks on the treadmill are running slow today. Run, you little devils ... speed it up ... run faster, or I'll cut off your nuts!"

Snow Job

SKI REPORT: "There is so little snow on the slopes in Salem, Oregon, this year that the long lines aren't for the lifts. They are to see the snowmen. There is so little snow this year, the snowmen are only made with two balls ... uh, normally, of course, snowmen have three balls ... there's no way in the world I can pull that one out of the fire. I'll just shut up while I'm behind."

Love Match

On NBC during the 4th set, Game 3, of the Wimbledon finals, after a terrific volley by Connors and Borg, Sportscaster Bud Collins said, "It seems anything you can do, I can do harder."

Try It . . . You'll Like It

Al Jolson was interviewed about prohibition on his return from Europe, and he momentarily forgot he was on the air. He was asked about the liquor situation in Europe and replied, "English beer tastes like warm cow piss."

Can't Win 'Em All

SPORTSCASTER: "The big news in sports is the Eagles' big win over the Bagels, Beagles . . . CINCINNATI BENGALS!"

Lover Boy

DISC JOCKEY: "And now from Paul Simon, '50 Ways to Love Your Liver.' "

Hairy Story

Heard on the "Cross Wits" game show:

EMCEE: That's the biggest mustache I have ever seen. Did you dye it yourself?"

CONTESTANT: "No, it's the same color as my hair all over my body."

Topsy Turvy

KARD, Channel 3, in Wichita, Kansas, was just beginning its new day of television broadcasting. The announcer said, "Good morning! Please join KARD as it begins another fine day of superb television entertainment." While this announcement was being made, on the screen was the identification card for the station. The card was upside down.

Keep on the Grass

During a New York Mets TV broadcast, the sportscaster was interviewing the president of the company that installed the artificial turf, and he said, "I'd take grass any day."

A Bird in His Hand Was Worth Two in the Bush

On "To Tell the Truth" the panel was to identify which of the three gentlemen present was the trainer of parakeets. When it came time for the panel to make their selection, the following dialogue took place:

BILL CULLEN: "I must disqualify myself. I met the correct gentleman in the rest room before the performance."

PEGGY CASS: "Well, yes, but how do you know it was the right man?"

BILL CULLEN: "Well, he had his bird in his hand!"

I Dig

"News Scene," Channel 7, San Francisco: Commentator Valerie Coleman on the 11 o'clock edition of the news said, "Today there was a very dig bug brust ... brug dust ... excuse me ... a very big bust!"

Paging Women's Lib

Arthur Godfrey, doing a Lipton Tea commercial on CBS, said, "When you are through with your old bag, just discard her, er, I mean tea bag!"

Under the Miss-eltoe

In the forties, when Bob Hope had a radio program, he had Jane Russell as a guest on a show during the Christmas holidays. Hope said to Russell, "Come here under the Christmas tree and kiss me under the balls." They were cut off the air pronto.

Put Them All Together They Spell Mother

"Monday Night Football" on ABC-TV sponsored a pass, punt, and kick contest for youngsters for half time entertainment. One fellow was named Darrell, and after the announcer introduced him, a spectator near an open mike yelled, "Atta boy, Darrell! Toss that muthah!"

Sick-Religious

This interchange took place between Bob Grant and a caller on Grant's WNBC radio talk show.

CALLER: (In a low hoarse voice) "You know, I see guys smoking at all the colleges around New York. Anywhere—Queens, St. Johns . . ."

GRANT: "Really, I can't believe that!"

CALLER: "Oh, yeah! I think pot is really invigorating, far out, it really stimulates my nerves. It's really a religious experience."

GRANT: "Religious! What the hell do you want to be when you grow up? ARCHBISHOP!"

Play by Play

About 30 years ago a wedding ceremony was being broadcast over a Springfield, Ohio, station. The announcer, describing the proceedings in hushed and awed tones, finally said, "And now the couple is approaching the altar where they will consummate the marriage."

A Stiff Question

Tony Randall was chatting with Johnny Carson on "The Tonight Show." Tony was talking about how his adrenalin rises as he is about to go on, and he blooped, "How do you get it up?"

Chance Remark

Disc jockey Sybil Chance of WXBM, Milton, Florida, blooped, "Here's George Jones singing 'In the Diarrhea of My Mind' . . . I'm sure that must be 'DIARY OF MY MIND'!"

I'll Take Navy

On WGBS, Miami, Florida, during a commercial for a manufacturer of tailor-made seat covers, the announcer concluded, "So see Johnny and Mack for the best in sailor-made teat covers in all fashionable colors."

The Iceman Cometh

On a Portland, Oregon, TV station there is a local commercial for a food manufacturing company featuring recipes called "Quickies in the Kitchen." The commercial announcer exhorted his viewers to watch a quickie in the kitchen!

Could Be

At WMAK in Nashville, Tennessee, Dave Steere concluded his commercial for the Old Maxwell House Hotel restaurant with, "So have dinner tonight at the Maxwell House restaurant. You'll never live to regret it!"

Up in Arms

NEWSCASTER: "Here is tonight's headline: 'PAIR CONVICTED OF ROBBED ARMORY.' "

Who's on First?

Heard on a daytime soap opera:

MINISTER: "Do you, Mike, take Beth as your lawfully wedded husband?"

Nice Trick if You Can Do It

Heard on "Perry Mason": "You may leave as you're going out."

Hear, Hear

A local television personality on WKYT-TV in Lexington, Kentucky, was previewing the events of the next day and explained that tomorrow's show would be interpreted for the deaf. She said, "So all of you watching, call all of your deaf friends and tell them to watch tomorrow morning. Thanks for listening."

Give Him the Gong

On "The Gong Show," Chuck Barris said, "And right now they live on a fairy farm ... DAIRY FARM!!"

A Come Back

WOCO radio, Oconto, Wisconsin, reported a murder-suicide. "The police stated that this was caused by the man shooting and killing himself, then proceeding to kill the young girl."

Hello, Dolly

Veteran newsman Lowell Thomas has become legendary for his uncontrollable laughter when something strikes him funny. The following is the verbatim transcript of one of his classic break ups.

THOMAS: " ... About a new book called *Diet or Die*. Author Mrs. Celeste Geyer, perhaps better known to millions of carnival fans as the one-time Dolly Dimples. Remember, the world's most beautiful fat lady? That was the billing Mrs. Geyer used when she weighed 555 pounds. Now a svelte 122, she tells in her book how she did it, following the advice of a doctor who told her after a near fart ... fartal heart attack to diet or die. (BREAKING UP) The secret to effective weight loss is massive willpower says Mrs. Geyer, adding that her own willpower was strengthened by ... (MORE BREAK UP) ... well, anyhow, she said that her fat friends from carnival life died at an early age and were later buried from the back of a truck. (COMPLETE BREAK UP) Why a truck? Because, said Mrs. Geyer, they were too big for a hearse." (COMPLETELY DESTROYED)

ANNOUNCER: "And so long until Monday, Lowell. (BREAK-ING UP) Listen each evening at this same time for the distinctive news reports of Lowell Thomas."

Really Big

NEWSCASTER: "Dolly Parton, country-western singer, has been nominated for an Emmy for two supporting roles . . . of course, I mean for her appearances on the Carol Burnett and Cher shows."

A Ringer

My research editor, Meredith Conover, spotted this Blooper. John Chancellor, anchorman for the "NBC Nightly News," told surprised viewers, "Jimmy Carter played a savage match against Vitas Gerulaitis at Wimbledon, Jimmy Connors, that is."

Quick on the Drawers

A contestant was telling about his wife's having a lot of wigs and spending so much money on them. He said, "My wife has more hair in her drawers than she has on her head."

A Bad Spell of Weather

Newsman Jim O'Brien on WPVI-TV, Philadelphia, was talking about a fast-moving weather system coming across the country. It was pushing out a bad weather system, which was moving half-assed.

Hep Cat

On a Worcester radio station, Jeff Starr was discussing cats, and he said, "A big cat can get you in a lot of trouble, but a little pussy never hurt anyone." He was fired the next day.

Seek and Ye Shall Find

On "The Liar's Club," when Jim McKrell was trying to describe
an object, he said, "This is the first thing Alex Haley found when
he was searching for his root."

Line Forms to the Right

On WCBS-FM Jim Harrington said, "For anyone who is interested, there will be free breast and uterine exhibitions, er, exam-
inations, located on Broadway at 11th Street in New York City."

Foot in Mouth

The Ohio State football team had a very fine point-after-touch-down kicker named Max Schnitker. On the 6:15 sports program the sports announcer said, "The extra point was made by Max Shitnicker, er, I mean, Shitkicker!"

Freudian Slip

On "Good Morning, America," John Coleman was describing the weather around the country and said, "The high tempera-tures will include 70 degrees in Las Wages."

Stop, Leak, and Listen

During the Watergate hearings a commentator intimated that Daniel Schorr might have persuaded an official to leak some information. After a commercial, the commentator said, "And now back to Daniel Schorr and his leak."

Teeny Wiener

On a children's news program the commentator said, "The gov-ernment has complained to the Wiener King Company in Chi-cago, Illinois, that their foot-long hot dog actually was not 12 inches long, but 10 inches." The announcer continued saying, "Of course, everyone knows Dodger Stadium sells foot-long hot dogs so you better watch out, Mr. O'Malley; you're in trouble if your wiener is not long enough."

Weirdo

On "Match Game, P.M." emcee Gene Rayburn asked a female contestant where she was from. She answered, "Hollyweird."

Silly Ass

On "The Swap Shop Show" on CKCW radio in Canada, a call came in, "For sale: one used roll of toilet paper." The DJ, who was obviously having a rough day, cut him off and said, "All right, smart ass . . . ."

Pointed Remark

Carol Burnett was a guest on "The Mike Douglas Show." They were talking about how this lady could hold up a strapless dress. Carol said she had asked the lady how she held it up, to which the lady answered, "If you had what I have, your dresses would stay up too." Mike replied, "That's really getting to the point."

It Figures

A commercial for a spaghetti sauce compared two brands. One brand was said to have no meat in it, only meat flavoring. The second brand was said to contain 3 times as much meat. Thus, in multiplication $3 \times 0 = 0$ so the second brand also had no meat!

Hot Stuff

NEWSMAN: "The blaze, which almost completely destroyed the building, was caused by an overheated hair dresser . . . ah . . . hair dryer!"

Blooper Award

During the Academy Awards one of the excited winners blooped, "... and least but not last I would like to thank ..."

Vasectomy

DISC JOCKEY: "And now we will have an hour of music by the orchestra of Sterile Stapleton ... that should by Cyril."

Paging Anita Bryant

During a commercial for a fruit-flavored cereal, Wilma Flint-stone remarked that there was a Fruitosaurus on the loose and that they'd better run for their lives because "he's searching for something fruity."

Out in the Fresh Air

During a Public Service announcement for the March of Dimes, the announcer said, "Now, I want all of you boys and girls to go out and fart ... (SILENCE) ... FIGHT for the March of Dimes."

Double Talk

When Frank Gifford described the dive that Pat Sucher was going to do from 148 feet, he said, "Pat is attempting to do a dummer subblesalt ... double sobersault!"

Porno Flick

ANNOUNCER: "Be sure to see the movie *Susan Slept Here* with Dick Powell this afternoon at 3:30."

Two Balls, One Strike

During a telecast of a New York Mets–St. Louis Cardinal game, the umpire behind home plate was wired with a mike. The St. Louis batter fouled a ball back that hit Mets' catcher Jerry Grote in the groin. Grote could be heard saying, "God damn, that mother hurt!"

Racy

During the Indy 500, Jim McKay described Johnny Rutherford's pit stop as a tit spot.

Jocular Remark

On "The Match Game," the question was: "The coach went into the locker room, and the team was holding a blank." The contestant said, "Jock rally." Panelist Brett Sommers said, "They were holding their balls."

Blessed Event

One Easter Sunday morning on WHBC AM-FM, Canton, Ohio, Tom Morrison, the duty announcer, was reading the news and made the following transposition: "The Pope appeared on the balcony of the Vatican Palace and blessed 10,000 Peters in St. People's Square."

Si, Senor

When Charo was a guest on "The Tonight Show," guest host Joey Bishop asked her to say the tongue twister, "She says she shall sew bed sheets." Charo, with her accent, said, "She says she shall sew bad shits." Joey recommended that she try saying "She says she shall sew pillow cases."

Lordy

NEWSMAN: "The report was attributed to Lord Snowden, the estranged wife of Princess Margaret . . . ."

A Clean Show

Dinah Shore, describing the TV show "All's Fair," starring Bernadette Peters, said, "The show is about two reporters who fall in love while washing in Workington, D.C."

Using His Noodle

Howard Cosell reported that in 1958 the Kentucky Derby was won by Noodles . . . NEEDLES!

A Hard Act to Follow

DISC JOCKEY: "Now let's listen to 'A Hard Man's Man,' . . . I mean . . . 'A Hard Woman's Woman,' . . . no, I mean . . . 'A Hard Woman's Man.' Welcome to goof night here on 590, CKEY Radio Toronto!"

A Bargain

A furniture commercial and an advertisement for a "Martin Luther King Special" were jumbled together in the same time slot. As it came out, the picture was of a living room set with the price slashed out, and the voice was that of Martin Luther King during his famous speech saying, "Free at last, free at last!"

Hokus Pokus

During "The Price Is Right" shell game, Bob Barker said, "Now I want you to tell me which ball the shell is under."

A Pregnant Thought

On the game show "Gambit," host Wink Martindale said, "Mrs. Baldwin is in labor ... uh ... that should be, she works for the Department of Labor."

A Passing Remark

On "Monday Night Football" on ABC, sportscaster Frank Gifford described "a quick piss to the left."

Where There's Life ... There's Hope

Let's tune in an early Bob Hope radio show when he became the victim of this unintended Blooper:

HOSTESS: "I'll bet you were frightfully upset."

HOPE: "Not ole Rob. Not me. I just cooked my cock ... (Audience hysteria) Cocked my pinkie! ... What did I say? Oh, I'd like to get a fresh start on the whole day."

No Kidding

ANNOUNCER: "This is a Public Service announcement. We urge you to participate in child abuse."

For Pete's Sake

After Cincinnati Red Pete Rose's remarkable hitting streak was halted, he was interviewed by the press. One reporter asked Pete if he was relieved. Pete snapped back with "I am pissed off!"

If at First You Don't Succeed ...

FRANK BLAIR (" Today Show "): " Lieutenant General Nguyen Van Thieu, Chief of State and military candidate for President, finally showed up at a rally with the civilian candidates. That story from Charles Murphy in South Vietnam. (NO REPORT) That story from Charles ... not quite ready yet. In the meantime, at the Lake of the Ozarks in Missouri, the annual meeting of the Midwestern Governor's Conference opens today. For a report here is Don Oliver at the Conference. (NO REPORT) Well, we will have that report a little later, too. This story I am sure that I can handle myself. The so-called Torch of Peace is moving slowly across the continent from San Francisco this morning in the hands of a team of relay runners. It's a peace campaign of a new kind. That story from John Dancy in San Francisco. (NO REPORT) You're kidding ... well, we'll have *that* story a little later on. I hope that we find time for all these things. There's news from Italy that will surprise no one. Some people are genuinely allergic to work. According to a report submitted to a conference on allergies, muscular activity on the part of those afflicted by work releases an extra amount of histamines, a stimulant that causes rashes and allergies. With a newscast like this, I'm getting more allergic every minute. Are we going to try for some of these stories now? Okay, we're ready. Over the weekend, as we told you, General Nguyen Van Thieu, who is one of the presidential candidates in Vietnam, finally started some campaigning with the civilians, and here is that story now from Charles Murphy in South Vietnam. (NO REPORT) Well, what page do you want, Larry? Do the weather? Well, okay, we probably won't get the weather map this time."

Go Man Go!

Don Knotts appeared as a guest with Dinah Shore. Don left the program during a commercial to fulfill a previous engagement. Don Meredith, who also was a guest asked, "What happened to Don?" Dinah replied, "Don Knotts had to go."

In Living Black and White

NEWSCASTER: "President Jimmy Carter will meet with white leaders in the Black House."

No Dice

SPORTSCASTER: "In Montreal, Canada, the United States received a gold medal in crapshooting ... trap shooting."

Junk

During the CBS Special, "In Celebration of U.S.," which featured coverage of "Operation Sail," showing great sailing ships, famed opera star Beverly Sills told Walter Cronkite that she saw a Chinese "junkie."

A Touchy Subject

When Steve Lawrence and Eydie Gorme were guests on "The Dinah Show," Eydie said, "I have a brown thumb. Everything I touch doesn't grow." Steve replied, "I wouldn't touch that with a ten-foot pitchfork!"

If I Knew You Were Coming, I'd Have Baked a Cake

Heard on "The Eleven O'Clock News": "President Ford had nothing to do with the Watergreat bake in."

I'm Game

A newscaster of KSYM-FM radio in Joplin, Missouri, startled his listeners with the following announcement: "Now we are going to play 'Forbidden Games.' (BREAKING UP) Of course, I meant the instrumental selection titled 'Forbidden Games'! "

Wartime

Frank McGee on "The Today Show" was interviewing someone about the war in Vietnam. When he was through with the interview, he said, "It is now 45 minutes past the war."

Lady of the Evening

NEWSCASTER: "The fire was promptly extinguished last night by Hooker and Ladder Company 69."

Dead Head

During the "11 O'Clock News" broadcast over WMAR-TV, Channel 2, Baltimore, reporter George Collins reported on the robbery of a gas station and the shootout that followed. He reported that the robber had died due to the officer's bullet, which hit him in the head and killed him dead.

That's the Way It Is

A Washington, D.C., promo advertised a special news feature in which a rookie basketball player was to "go one-on-one with sportscaster Mike Wolfe." However, a tape was prematurely aired, and the viewers heard, "The rookie will go one-on-one with (CUT IN) Walter Cronkite and 'The CBS Evening News.'"

So What Else Is New?

Performers on talk shows very often try to think of their next question before listening to the answer to the question already asked. A classic example occurred on "The Dinah Show." Dinah was asking Walter Matthau in what order did he put health, sex, and money when he was young. He said that sex didn't mean that much then because he didn't lose his virginity until he was 24. Then Dinah, thinking about the next question, asked him if it was fun.

A Fish Story

Tony Jacobs of WCBI Radio in Columbus, Missouri, reports about his first job in radio. This resulted in his first live commercial, which, in turn, resulted in his first live Blooper concerning a restaurant that specialized in pan-fried catfish. He asked, "Have you ever eaten can-fried patfish on the shores of a bootiful lake?"

Crash Program

On a Columbus, Ohio, TV station a local furniture company entices customers by offering merchandise for only nine cents with the purchase of a furniture suite. During a live commercial the announcer remarked, "... and you get this beautiful, *sturdy* chest of drawers for only nine cents ... that's right, only nine cents." He then moved his arm in a sweeping motion, just barely touching the chest of drawers with his hand—but that was enough. There was a creaking noise followed by the crashing collapse of the dresser. The announcer just stared at the heap in embarrassed disbelief after which he ad libbed, "I wanted to be sure you were paying attention."

Ball Player

One evening during the 1972 Olympics, during preparation for a men's swimming race, one young man was shown thrusting his hand into the front of his trunks in order to rearrange his accouterments. No comment was made, nor was the camera cut away.

Pop-Corn

DISC JOCKEY: "Here's something originally done by the Carpenters called 'We've Only Just Begun' ... this time being played by Arthur Pops and the Boston Fiedler ... (BREAKING UP) ... that should be Arthur Fiedler and the Boston Pops!"

Call a Cop

Les Real, the Public Safety Department's personnel director, guested on a WINZ, Miami, talk show to discuss recruitment. Asked if there were maternity benefits, he answered in the affirmative, noting that, "A number of our policewomen have gotten pregnant on the job."

A Honey of a Story

On a KKEY, Portland, Oregon, talk show a woman phoned the station.

HOST: "Good afternoon, you're on KKEY."

CALLER: "Hello, I'm a woman, Honey."

HOST: "I would not have guessed that ... and I'm not your 'Honey'!"

The caller kept calling the host "Honey." He became annoyed and warned that he would turn her off if she didn't stop calling him "Honey." She called him "Honey" again, so the host cut the caller off. The station had a commercial about endangered species during which over an open mike, he could be heard laughing and remarking, "Wasn't I a bastard? If there is anything I can't stand, it is to be called horny ... I mean, 'Honey.' "

It Can't Hurt

On Philadelphia's "Channel 10 News" program, anchorman Ralph Penza announced, "Some people in New England are setting up chicken soap kittens to help fight the flu ... uh, that should be chicken soap kitchens ... SOUP!!"

You Don't Have to Be Jewish

On a "Liberty Bowl" football telecast, the sportscasters were Keith Jackson and Frank Royals. It was near the end of the first half when Nebraska was marching down the field. On a 4th down play, North Carolina stopped them short by inches, which prompted Keith Jackson, referring to golf, to remark to Frank, "Just like you, left your putts two inches short." Being gentiles, neither of them realized that "putz" in Yiddish is the male organ.

A Little White Lie

On "The Liar's Club" game show shown on WMAR-TV, celebrities are given a gadget of some sort and have to tell what it is, one telling the truth and the rest lying. The contestants have to guess who is telling the truth. It was the final round of play when host Allen Ludden turned to Larry Hovis and said, "Larry, hold up your little thing and describe it." After the laughter died down, he began to describe the object (a tablecloth clip which he was passing off as a screendoor bumper) by saying, "Well, it's white and sort of springy!"

The Sun Never Sets

WEATHER FORECASTER: "Partly cloudy today with a high of 45 degrees. Tonight it will be partly sunny with a low of 59 degrees with very little weather expected."

Get Out of Town

On a John Denver Special, "An Evening with John Denver," he was telling a story about a song he sings called "Saturday Night in Toledo, Ohio." While he was in Toledo, he wanted to sing that song even though it was rather insulting to the town. He put it this way, "I couldn't passibly piss up the chance to sing that song!"

When You Gotta Go . . . You Gotta Go!

On "Match Game '76" when the TV station was fading to a commercial, panelist Brett Sommers could be heard saying, "I have to go to the bathroom."

Tricky Dick

On "The $20,000 Pyramid" Dick Cavett was trying to make the contestant say the word "rubbers." He tried with clues like "You put them over your shoes," without success. Finally, he said, "Male contraceptives." The contestant got the word right away.

Fall Guy

Orchestra leader Lawrence Welk asked one of the ladies in the audience to square dance with him. As the music went faster, so did Lawrence Welk and the woman, until finally they went around so fast that her wig flew off. The audience broke up, the lady quickly disappeared, and all Welk could ad lib was, "Well, there are a few surprises once in a while on this show."

When the Swallows Come Back

NEWSCASTER: "His battalion was swallowed in the Bulging Belch ... I beg your pardon ... I mean, the Belgian Bulge!"

Six of One—Half a Dozen of the Udder

This happened during on-the-spot coverage of a flood. The announcer watched a cow in the middle of the rising river. "There's a cow out in the water, and the water is up to her ..." His memory slipped, and he couldn't think of the word "udder." He revamped his description, "Well, she's deep in the water with the milk still on top."

Whatcha Know, Joe?

Ham Fisher, the celebrated cartoonist of Joe Palooka, was introduced thus: "And as anchor man on our panel tonight, we have the nation's number one cartoonist, the creator of Joe Falooka . . . Mr. Ham Pisher!"

No Substitutions, Please

Tommy Dixon, announcer of "Quiz of Two Cities," remembers a home economics program he was emceeing for KHJ with Norma Young. The phrase was "cracked crab salad." Three times it came out "crapped crap salad." He finally had to serve lettuce and tomatoes and let it go at that.

Extra Extra . . . Read All about It

Heard on "The Eleven O'Clock News": ". . . was phemoamal . . . pheomelel . . . phenelemen . . . oh, heck . . . extraordinary!"

Special Delivery

Peter Donald, when emceeing "Guess Who" on the Mutual Network, asked, "What do you do for a living?" The contestant answered, "I go around picking up ladies' dresses." When the roar of laughter from the audience died down, he learned that the contestant worked as a delivery man for a tailor!

All in the Family

Heard on a daytime TV soap opera: "We heard a car driving speedily up the dirt road ... it stopped with a jerk ... my nephew Percy got out."

Fill 'Er Up

When Ed Wynn was the Texaco Fire Chief, Graham McNamee, one of the truly great announcers of all time, did the commercial for Texaco. Ed Wynn kidded Graham for weeks after McNamee reminded his millions of listeners, "When you see the famous sign of the Fire Chief, fill up with Texagoo gasaloon."

Convenience Store

ANNOUNCER: "The Calgery Drug and Rape Shop is on the air . . . Rug and Drape Shop!"

Quick on the Drawbridge

Robin Chandler on "Quick on the Draw" said, "As the bridge was about to be raised, he hurried to get a broad a Staten Island fairy."

The Lowdown

Sometimes an actor, without realizing it, will improve a script. Once on a gangster show two crooks had kidnapped the governor's daughter. One warned the other, "Look, Al, we gotta low lay here . . . lay low here!"

Please Don't Squeeze the Charmin

On "Sense and Nonsense," an NBC-TV audience participation program, Bob Kennedy, the popular emcee, asked a contestant to identify a certain object by a sense of smell. The object was a freshly printed newspaper. While the contestant, a youngster of ten, knew immediately that it was paper, he was uncertain as to what kind. Kennedy, by way of a hint, suggested that, "This has a very special odor." This immediately dispelled a cloud of doubt in the young contestant's mind who unhesitatingly answered, "Toilet paper!"

Knots to You

WEATHER MAN: "The marine weather forecast shows winds southeast at 65 miles per hour demolishing this afternoon."

Flowery Language

Harry Balogh, who introduced the prize fighters from Madison Square Garden, blooped the following on national television: "... in this corner, one of America's foremost fistic gladiolas ... er ... gladiators ... weighing 201 pounds ...."

Looking Good

The following was heard on a live daytime soap opera: "The woman was tall, manure, and teatly dressed."

Did You Notice Anything Unusual?

ACTOR: "The only clue that we have is that the suspect wore hornrimmed testicles."

A Quick-ie Recovery

This Blooper occurred on the "Young Doctor Malone" radio program: "His wife awaited a report about her husband who was in bed with a nurse."

All Shook Up

On an early morning fund raiser for station KAXE-FM in Grand Rapids, Michigan, Marie Janecek, a volunteer at the station, was expounding on the merits of the station when she became startled by an outside explosion. This is what the listeners heard: "The nice thing about KAXE is that you will most likely wake up to . . . Oh, my God, what's that!?!"

Country Boy

During the "Donny and Marie Special" (Marie's 18th birthday), Donny and Marie traded positions during the "concert spot." Donny sang country music while Marie sang rock music. After the various songs had been sung, Donny usually sings "She's a little bit country . . . ," but this night he forgot they had traded places until he sang, "She's a little bit . . . ," stopping himself in the middle of the word *country*.

The Jerk

On radio station WLEC, Sandusky, Ohio, the station presents eerie Edgar Allan Poe stories and ghost stories on Halloween. Program Director Karl Bates presides over the proceedings and bills himself as "Your Master of Suspense." Following a commercial, the announcer turned the program back to Karl with the words, "And now, Master Bates."

Wash His Mouth Out with Soap

The announcer ended each of the soap opera segments with "And thus endeth another version of today's story." The program ran a few seconds over as he closed, "And thus endeth another virgin . . ."

Honesty Is the Best Policy

NEWSCASTER: "The price of strawberries, as well as the price of many other fruits and vegetables, is bound to be higher from now on. Bill Stout, CBS News, Selenus, California." (STOUT, BELIEVING HE IS OFF CAMERA, TAKES A BITE OF STRAWBERRY, GRIMACES, AND SPITS IT OUT.)

Dead or Alive

President Johnson's press adviser, Bill Moyers, had this information to pass along to amused news reporters. "Off the record and for your guidance, there will be a surprise disaster drill at the hospital tomorrow at 10:00 A.M. (BREAK UP) I am advising you of this because the hospital will have sixty simulated casualties. (BREAK UP) The hospital says that this is a serious business, and they wanted you to know, off the record, that this is going to happen. Photographers will be welcome. (COMPLETE BREAK UP) The press should be advised that the sixty casualties will be simulated and not White House staff!" (COMPLETELY OUT OF CONTROL)

Collision Course

NEWSCASTER: "The single engine Navy fighter collided with what was apparently a buzzard. The pilot was forced to eject. He parachuted to safety. Navy authorities in Jacksonville ... (BREAK UP) ... I can't see this plane hitting a buzzard. (UNCONTROLLABLE LAUGHTER) A fantastic story in Florida today when a single engine Navy fighter (BREAK UP) on a routine ... (UNCONTROLLABLE LAUGHTER) ... Navy authorities in Jacksonville say that Lieutenant Schwartz ..." (UNABLE TO CONTINUE)

He's Got Plenty of Nuttin'

In his anxiety to please his new sponsor, Chock Full O' Nuts, Morey Amsterdam tripped over the client's name and spurted out, "You will enjoy a Jock Full O' Nuts special."

A Winner

Just before the prizefight, Harry Balogh, the chief announcer at Madison Square Garden, wished the two contenders luck by saying, "May the winner emerge victorious."

The Straw That Broke the Camel's Back

W. C. Fields committed this hilarious boner. It happened years ago in Hollywood when Fields was being interviewed on a Camel cigarette program. Throughout the course of the interview, he kept referring to his son, Chester Fields, and didn't realize the embarrassment of the program's sponsors. When the program was over, his interviewer told him that he mentioned his son, Chester Fields, at least nine times, much to the consternation of the emcee who was ready to walk a mile.

Bottoms Up

At the launching of the *Queen Mary,* one of His Majesty's proudest luxury liners, a British Broadcasting announcer made this observation, "From where I am standing, I can see the Queen's bottom sticking out just over her waterline."

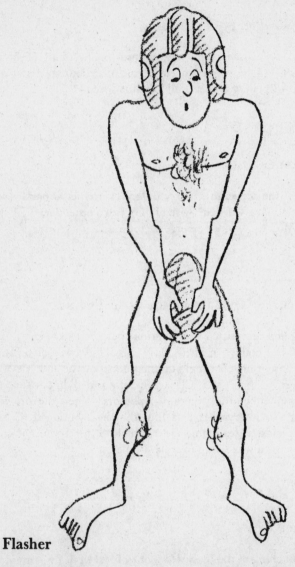

Flasher

SPORTSCASTER: "It's a naked reverse. The quarterback has the ball; he is running around his own end and is now standing naked in the end zone."

Wolf Man

Bill Cullen, popular emcee and panelist, was interviewing a luscious blonde from the deep South whose correct answer would win her a dress as her prize. When the contestant was greeted by wolf whistles from the audience, Bill started the usual teasing about her beauty, Southern drawl, and the many rich endowments nature bestowed on her. The young lady, becoming impatient as she was intent upon winning this dress, drawled, "Why, Mr. Cullen, are you all tryin' to talk me outa mah dress?"

Regular Guy

On "Hobby Lobby," one of radio's early programs, Stepin Fetchit, the black, slow-talking comedian, was a guest hobbyist. Fetchit was a collector of dice from all over the world and had in his possession dice from Nick the Greek to the crowned heads of Europe. Dave Elman, program emcee, rolled a pair of dice several times, and each time the number seven showed up. Fetchit said, "Mistuh Elman, if youse keeps on usin' dese, youse'll craps regular!"

Bodies by Fisher

Ham Fisher, celebrated cartoonist, was a guest judge on the TV beauty contest series to select "Miss New York Television." Ted Steele, popular TV personality, was the emcee, and it was his custom to conduct a brief interview with the judges. Steele asked Fisher how he liked the girls. Fisher fluffed, "With all the feminine pulchritude around the studio, I have to grasp for breast . . . I mean, gasp for breath!!"

He Could Spit

Milton Cross was known as the Dean of Announcers. His broadcasts from the Metropolitan Opera House in New York have been heard worldwide for many years.

CROSS: "And now the house lights are dimming, a hush falls over the expectorant audience as our Maestro, the well-known American conductor, makes his way to the podium."

What Kind of Fool Am I?

Erskine Johnson, Hollywood commentator, was broadcasting over a Los Angeles station. He was well into his script when he was suddenly stopped cold by the voice of the producer who had come out of the booth and into the studio. "I can't stand this stuff night after night," he screamed. Johnson's eyes nearly fell out of his head, but he kept on reading. "How can YOU read this crap every night?" the producer demanded. Johnson, sure the man had gone mad, kept on, waiting for the announcer to lead him away to the wagon, which must be waiting. Instead the announcer took up where the producer left off, and between them, they outscreamed Johnson. Finally, at the end of his broadcast, Johnson laid down his script and believed his radio career had ended. It wasn't until they both burst out laughing that Erskine realized that it was April first!

Pooped!

Thaine Engle, former Audience Promotion Supervisor of NBC, tells us this one, made while he was an announcer at WBAP, Fort Worth, Texas. He was supposed to say, "Don't forget to ask for Pepperel Red Label Sheets," only it came out, "Don't forget to ask for Pooperell Red LABOR Sheets."

Three's a Cloud

Merv Griffin was introducing his guest Frankie Laine. The introduction was as follows: "Frankie is always a cloud peaser ... I mean, crowd pleaser."

Rural Delivery

EMCEE: "And now, ladies, it's your turn to choose how they will answer some of 'Newlywed Game's' ten-point questions, so here's your first question. Kathy, will your husband say that he is more basically urban or rural?"

KATHY: "I don't know what they mean."

EMCEE: "You know him well. What do you think?"

KATHY: "Heck ... he's more urban."

EMCEE: "He's urban. How long has he been that way?"

KATHY: "For about two months." (AUDIENCE LAUGHTER)

EMCEE: "For about two months he's been that way. Do you think that there is anything that he can do about it?"

KATHY: "He went to a doctor."

EMCEE: "Oh, he did? Did the doctor give him anything for his urban?"

KATHY: "He gave me something."

(AUDIENCE HYSTERIA)

Paging the Censor

David Ross, veteran announcer, noted for his poetic readings, had his audience chuckling with the following: "I would like to read an immoral poem, er, I mean, immortal poem."

Oh Mein Pappa

Bob Tomlinson, KGW's chief announcer, interviewed a four-year-old youngster participating in the annual Portland "Rose Festival Parade" some years ago. Bob asked, "What's your daddy's name?" to which the little girl replied, "Do you want my daddy's name or my momma's boyfriend's?"

Pickled

From KRLC, Lewiston, Idaho, comes this Blooper. Norm Mann, reading a commercial in which there was the phrase "tickled pink," said, "Your daughter will be tickled pick . . . pinckled tick . . . pickled tink."

Topper

Eleanor Roosevelt ad libbed the following during a press interview: "In our intercourse with other nations, may we always come out on top."

Better Dead Than Red

Wild Bill Hickok had his program interrupted by a newscaster just after four shots were fired by the program's sound-effects man. Here's how it went. "We interrupt this program to bring you a bulletin from the Mutual Newsroom. L. P. Beria has just been executed, according to an announcement from Moscow Radio. We now return you to 'Wild Bill Hickok'." At that moment, Guy Madison was reading his line. "Well, that should hold him for awhile."

Knock Knock

ANNOUNCER: "At Layton's you will find a pair of beautiful knockers ... pardon me ... I mean, knickers, for your husband."

Yankee, Go Home

NEWSCASTER: "Governor Rockefeller is on his last legs of his mission in Latin America for President Nixon."

Good Seats

An emcee of a radio show noticed that his announcer's mother and her granddaughter, both named Fanny, were in the audience. In the course of conversation on the air, he said, "Well, I see we have in our audience today two FANNYS in the front row."

Egg on Your Face

On a quiz show the question was, "How many eggs does a kiwi bird lay in one year?" After asking several women, the emcee repeated the question carelessly. "And how many kiwi birds would you say a kiwi bird laid in one year?" Then the emcee spent at least fifteen seconds shouting, "Eggs! Eggs! Eggs!"

Out of the Mouths of Babes

Art Linkletter to a 5-year-old: "What do people get married for?"

Answer: "To have fun making babies."

Tall Story

SPORTSCASTER: "Ladies and gentlemen, we are talking to the great Kansas University middle-distance runner and world's record holder in the mile, Jim Ryun. Jim is 3 foot 3 inches tall . . . wait a minute, something's wrong here . . . he's gotta be at least 6 feet tall!"

Comic Opera

ANNOUNCER: "We now hear the Victor Herbert selection, 'Ah, Sweet Mystery of Life,' to be sung by Metropolitan LIFE tenor Richard Tucker."

Highway Robbery

LOCAL NEWS: "The robbers got away in their automobile after taking only $11 from the gas station attendant .... Next time you're out driving ... why don't you take in a really good gas station ... Citgo."

Well Lit

TV sports announcer describing Army-Navy football game: "And Navy came onto the field with orange phosphorescent helmets on their ends."

A Bang-up Job

While the TV screen showed a pistol pointed at viewers for the opening of a Western, the audio portion asked, "What do doctors recommend for headaches?"

By Cracky

Bob Priddy was conducting his usual weekly program on water safety on KLIK, Jefferson City, Missouri. He asked his guest, "Ken, what should the average boat owner be doing at this time of year?" "Well, Bob," Ken replied, "they should be checking their bottoms for cracks."

Boys Will Be Boys

On a "Man Against Crime" TV episode concerning the basketball scandals of some years back, Ralph Bellamy was the lead on the show, which was done live. As Mike Barnett, he was hired by a college to look into possible skulduggery on the part of their basketball team. "You mean," said Bellamy in his best deadpan private-eye manner, "you want me to investigate the balls on the boys' club?" He looked into the camera for a painful few seconds and then somehow carried on.

Fizzled Commercial

At the end of a radio newscast, the commercial announcer for Alka-Seltzer said his usual, "Listen to it fizz," only to have a melodious clink ring out over the air. He had forgotten to put water in the glass!

Thrown a Curve

The following occurred on a local radio station in Safford, Arizona. The announcer was an inveterate ad libber. This particular morning he was late and was therefore reading cold copy. "Visit Ferguson's Firestone Store where they're having the greatest sale ever on new electric ranges. See these beautiful ranges, designed with smooth, sweeping curves (here he ad libbed) just like the girl next door." Unfortunately, there was nowhere else to go but back to the copy, the next line of which read, "no cracks or crevices in which to collect dirt or grease."

Good Night, Folks!

A disc jockey was signing off a show. He was searching for something different to say. He could not decide whether or not to say, "That's the whole shebang" or "That's the whole kit and caboodle." As it turned out, his indecision led him to say, "Well, that's the whole shittinkabootle!"

Nudie

NEWSCASTER: "A barge with two men and a girl abroad is adrift in the Delaway Bare area . . . the Delaware Bay area!"

From Soupy to Nuts

The following Blooper was committed by Soupy Sales when he told the kids about the new putty by Chloroform. After he rolled on the floor, stricken with laughter, he finally corrected himself by saying, "I meant Colorforms."

Juiced Up

An NBC announcer was giving a promo over a slide for "The Dr. Joyce Brothers Show." He started like this: "Tonight Dr. Juice Brewers . . . Tonight Dr. Juice Brothers' viewers will find out why . . ."

It's What's Up Front That Counts

Art Linkletter was interviewing children between the ages of six and seven. When he got to one little six-year-old girl, he asked what age she'd like to be. She responded, "Seventeen." Mr. Linkletter stated that was a very interesting age and asked her why she'd like to be that age. The little girl snapped back, "So I could wear a bra!"

Hand Off

Calling the play-by-play of a high school football game over WBYE, Calera, Alabama, the announcer was indeed excited. The home team had taken the opening kickoff and had ground out hard-won yardage. Recapping the drive, the announcer ended with the declaration, ". . . for the first time in this game, the Warriors have their balls in their hands . . . er, ah . . . I mean, their hands on the ball!"

Roots

A farm specialist once revealed this advice to his listeners. "If you think you have root rot, the best way to find out is to pull it out and look at it."

Here Comes the Mailman

"Kitchen Klatter" is a home economics program produced by a food flavoring firm in Shenandoah, Iowa. The emcee of the program told of how she likes to receive mail. "I like to go to bed at night with a handful of mail . . ." After some titters from the TV crew, she explained . . . "Okay, fellas, that's M-A-I-L!"

Pin the Tail ...

Xavier Cugat, popular Latin band leader, appeared with his new 19-year-old bride, Charo, on "The Merv Griffin Show." She spoke very little English. Both Merv and Henry Morgan, who was a guest on the program, tried to find out from her how and where she met "Cugie." She managed to tell them that when she first met him on the beach in Madrid, "He was with a beautiful ass." After much audience hysteria, Cugat cleared the matter up by telling the audience that he was riding a donkey.

Comic Strip

The following was heard on a children's TV show: "So remember, kids, tune in next week at the same time for another 'Let's Take a Strip' ... 'Let's Take a Trip Show'!! "

So Solly

NEWSCASTER: "The next news item concerns the impending marriage of Japan's Clown Prince ... CROWN PRINCE ... who will make ... I mean, take his bride on Thursday."

Party Time

DISC JOCKEY: "Here's Julie London 'Making Whoopie' ... that is Julie singing 'Making Whoopie.' "

Phone-a-Vision

Art Merrill, WIOD, Miami, telephone talk show host had this conversation with a female caller.

HOST: "Hello."

CALLER: "Hello, do you know who this is?"

HOST: "Oh, hello there."

CALLER: "How are you?"

HOST: "Okay."

CALLER: "I've been lying here in bed lately wondering what you look like."

HOST: "All right."

CALLER: "And I've come to the conclusion . . . I would say that you're about 6 feet tall, 155 pounds."

HOST: "Yeah, true so far."

CALLER: "Light brown hair. Am I right so far?"

HOST: "Yes."

CALLER: "You are very erect, that is, you stand very erect. I would think that you have a fairyish complexion."

HOST: "Fair."

CALLER: "I think that it would be great if we could see you exposed . . . I mean, in public."

HOST: (LAUGHING) "Well, I'm going up to a nudist colony on Sunday . . ."

(UNABLE TO CONTINUE, HE CUTS THE CALLER OFF.)

TV or Not TV . . . That Is the Question

Former President Gerald Ford in an interview at the ball park told sports fans, "I enjoy watching the Detroit Tigers on radio."

Sweet Talk

Wrestling announcer Paul Boesch was doing the commentary behind a live telecast of wrestling matches in Houston, Texas. His assistant had handed him a Coke, and he held the drink in one hand, and the mike in the other. As the match progressed, he kept his voice smooth by a sip of Coke here and there. Suddenly, he saw his sound man running toward him waving his arms. He had put the mike down and was talking into the bottle of Coke!

On the Hot Seat

PUBLIC SERVICE ANNOUNCEMENT: "This is your Texas Department of Public Safety urging listeners to prevent forest fires . . . . When you're out in a car, be sure to use your ass trays."

Ladies' Home Companion

DISC JOCKEY: "This is Martin Block spinning another record . . . this time, let's hear from the Mills Brothers singing 'Be My Wife's Companion!' . . . I beg your pardon . . . that should be 'Be My Life's Companion.' "

Call Girl

EMCEE: "Well, girls, that just about wraps up another telephone quiz program for tonight. This is Carl Forsgate asking that you tune in again tomorrow at the same time when I'll be crawling on you again!"

A Sinking Feeling

Burt Lance, being interviewed on ABC's "Good Morning, America," told the network audience, "We have a stinking stock market economy . . . er . . . SINKING!"

The Living End

COMMERCIAL: "So go to your neighborhood movie and see *Frankenstein,* starring Boris Karloff in a chiller-diller that is guaranteed to make your end stand on hair. Uh, that is, to make your end stand up!"

Funny Valentine

COMMERCIAL: "So drop in at Henry's roadside restaurant, where Sunday they are featuring a special Valentine's Day dinner for two dollars. Featured on the menu is a delicious best of breasts ... breasts of beast ... what I mean to say is breast of beef!"

Private Property

PUBLIC SERVICE ANNOUNCEMENT: "This is Pfc. Helen Miller of the U.S. Army Recruiting Corps. I want to tell you men that there is an opportunity for you with an insured future with the U.S. Army. The U.S. Army is known throughout the world for the care, training, and handling of its privates."

Cwayze, Man, Cwayze

"This is John Sameron Cwayze ... John Cameron Swayze in the ABC radio network newsroom in New York. From September 15 on, listeners will get the full benefit of the ABC radio network's worldwide nudes ... (OFF MIKE) Son of a bitch!"

Flexible Flyers

During the telecast of a fashion show that originated in New York, the fashion commentator tried to tell her audience something about the flags of all nations. "It's a beautiful day here in New York, and as we approach 50th Street and 5th Avenue, and as we look up above, we see the fags of all nations flying in the breeze."

Cuban Heel

A newscaster was carried away by the excitement of the Cuban invasion. He tried to tell his radio audience about the mobilization of anti-Castro forces. "Consensus of newsmen's opinions in Havana and Miami is that the people of Cuba are beginning to join antro-Castrate forces ... that should be anti-Castrate forces!!"

Duty Calls

Viewers of the popular "Zoorama" animal show were amused to witness this unplanned act of nature. "This is a member of the kangaroo family. Sometimes they have been known to drop dead when people have tried to catch them. Yet here she sits quietly on the doctor's lap. Join us on 'Zoorama' to learn why." (AS THE CAMERA PULLS AWAY, THE KANGAROO DROPS A LOAD.)

Good Night!!

"Good night, David, this is Chet Huntley for NPP News . . . NPC . . . NBC News!"

Golf Widow

EMCEE: "All right, madam, before we get down to the business at hand, I know you are anxious to win some prizes. I want you to tell our audience about your family and children."

ANSWER: "I haven't any children. My husband's hobby is golf."

Anti-Freeze

SPORTSCASTER: "Although chilly weather prevails at this Army-Navy classic, spirits are warming the fans at this renewal of a classic football rivalry."

Up, Up, and Away

Heard on the "Phil Donahue Show": For some men sex is a real hard job."

Razor Sharp

QUIZ PROGRAM: "All right, sir, the category you have chosen is biology. We want you to tell us what the Schick test is for."

ANSWER: "Shaving!"

Horsing Around

SPORTSCASTER: "And the horse owners are reminded to turn in their registration forms . . . they must do this because one copy goes to the Ohio Racing Commission and the other to the book-makers!! I mean, bookkeepers!"

Slow Burn

When I was in Baltimore in connection with my presentation of *Blunderful World of Bloopers,* a one-man, multimedia show at Johns Hopkins University, I also appeared as a guest on the Meryl Comer show, "2's Company," on WMAR-TV. Meryl showed me a videotape in which she was lip syncing a song when the tape began to slow down. Meryl slowed down her lip sync, much to her consternation!

The Show Must Go On

The following happened to Tom Snyder when he worked on a Philadelphia TV station. "Hello, this is Tom Snyder. Please join us for the 'Contact' program Thursday morning at nine o'clock. I'm falling." (SNYDER'S CHAIR FALLS OVER) From the floor he says, "It will be a great show!"

Boing!!

Presidential ceremonies don't always go as smoothly as seen on television. For instance, former President Nixon was walking toward his helicopter. "Hail to the Chief" was being played. The Marines rolled out the red carpet to the door of the plane. As one Marine bent to straighten the carpet, the helicopter door dropped down, clonking him on the head! In true Marine tradition, the Marine straightened his helmet, stood erect, and saluted his Commander-in-Chief.

Puppy Love

PUBLIC SERVICE ANNOUNCEMENT: "Have you always wanted a soft, fluffy kitten or a fat, cuddly puppy? Perhaps you don't have time to fuss with a baby animal and would prefer an adult dog or cat. The Humane Society of Greater Miami has many dogs or cats available for adoption. They're sure to have one that's just right for you. Visit the Humane Society of Greater Miami or the pet adoption center nearest you. The right pet can add new dimensions to your life." (PUPPY UPCHUCKS)

One on One

NEWSMAN JOHN SCALLI: "Does this plane run well on one engine?"

PILOT: "It runs best on one engine. That's all it has!!"

Ya Hoo!

On KOA, Denver, a newscaster told his audience, "Rita Hayworth is now reposing on a Nevada Nude Ranch ... DUDE RANCH!"

In Union There Is Strength

LOCAL NEWS: "And the farmers of Boynton County have banded together to form a protective chicken-stealing association ... (PAUSE) ... that sounds like they are doing the stealing ... of course, you know that is not what I mean!"

Brand Double X

Sports personality Harry Wismer was a guest on Dick Noel's sports program, which was sponsored by a cigarette company. As part of the commercial, Wismer was given a blindfold test. "This is a great cigarette," he said after taking a puff, "tastes wonderful." "Wait a minute, Harry," countered Noel, "you haven't tasted our brand yet."

A Sleeper

DISC JOCKEY: "And now a record by Little Willie John ... here's 'Sleep, Sleep, Sleep' ... By the way, did you get any last night? (PAUSE) ... SLEEP, that is!"

Ride 'Em Cowboy

STATION BREAK: "Stay tuned for another exciting adventure of 'Hore Ride' ... er ... 'RAWHIDE'!"

Safety First

Veteran announcer Frank Gallup found himself in this double entendre predicament while doing a commercial for the Prudential Life Insurance Company.

GALLUP: "Well, today I would like to tell you about a box. About a very special kind of box. Perhaps you own such a box yourself, and in it may be the same curious assortment of treasures. (BREAKING UP) Now if the owner of the box that I have in mind were to tell you about it, she would say something like this: 'Years ago when John and I were first married, (AUDIENCE LAUGHING) we bought ourselves what was called in those days a strong-box. The first things that we put in it were our marriage certificate and a few securities. (MORE BREAK UP) But as time passed, many kinds of things found their way into the box. (HYSTERIA) There was the orchid carefully pressed that John gave me on our anniversary, there was a lock of our baby's hair, some love letters, a service medal, a Purple Heart, and among these things the most meaningful treasure of all was John's Prudential Life Insurance.' (UNCONTROLLABLE LAUGHTER) Friends, Prudential makes it easier for a man to be foresighted. You see he doesn't have to depend on time and long, slow effort to create security for his family. Can you think of a safer, surer, more convenient way to protect your family?"

There's Many a Slip Twixt the Cup and the Lip

A spoonerism is an unintended interchange of syllables. The following is a classic example:

NEWSCASTER: "And the guests at the Saigon inauguration of President Van Thieu shit sampagne . . . shipped sampagne!"

Bowled Over

GENE RAYBURN: "Now a 'Monitor Sports' Special. Another report on the $100,000 All Star Bowling Tournament. Here's Sam Levine in Convention Hall in Philadelphia. (SILENCE) Well, I guess we are having a little problem with the storm or something. We can't get hold of Sam Levine. Is he there now? Okay, Sam, go."

LEVINE: "... In Philadelphia for 'Monitor Sports.'"

RAYBURN: "That's it? We are still going to try to get Sam Levine. I'm trying to figure out what is going on here. Fellows, are we going to try? Okay. When I say go, the next voice that you hear will be that of Sam Levine. Okay, Sam, go."

LEVINE: "... In Philadelphia for 'Monitor Sports.'"

RAYBURN: "Well, you can't win them all, friends."

Cloudy Specimen

NEWSCASTER: "The first step is the new meeting of European Common Market foreign ministers. Italy wants such a session in Venice starting on or about May 10. The Eurine Peein ... Euren peon ... political ... picture is cloudy ...."

Coming On Strong

ANNOUNCER: "For fun and excitement watch *Hercules on the Captured Women* ... I mean, *Hercules and the Captured Women!*"

Man-to-Man Talk

The following was heard on a conversation program on WWJ-TV in Detroit: "In France there is a store that has a unique service for men whose husbands are away."

Gone but Not Forgotten

Heard on KVFC in Cortez, Colorado: "We suggest that all our listeners get over to the high school tonight and see their production of *Auntie Gone.*" Voice off microphone: "That's *Antigone,* you imbecile!"

Little Ole Winemaker

The following incident happened on "Top of the Pops," a program originating from London over the BBC and carried live via early-bird satellite. Host Bryan Matthew introduced Wayne Fontana and the Mindbenders, an extremely popular English group. "And now, our first guests today are a young group who've risen to unanimous popularity in an amazingly short period of time. Ladies and gentlemen, Wino Fontana and the Winevenders. (SHRILLS OF LAUGHTER IN THE BACKGROUND) Whoops, well, nobody's perfect, terribly sorry about that, chaps!"

On the Go-Go

STATION PROMO: "Sam Levenson is host on 'The Tonight Show' while Johnny is on the Johnny ... while Johnny is on vacation in color!"

Bisexual

Phil Donahue had Frederick of Hollywood, the well-known designer of revealing lingerie, as a guest. They were showing the latest bathing suit fashions. Phil asked, "Are your designers male or female?" The reply was, "A combination of both."

Leap Year

SPORTSCASTER: "And now the time is coming up for the highlight of this intersectional track and field event—the girls' junior broad bumping championship."

Tennis, Anyone?

EMCEE: "All right, young lady, you have chosen the category of sports. If you guess the correct answer, you will take home this beautiful one-hundred-piece sterling silver flatware set. If you miss, you will get two tickets to your neighborhood movie theater .... At what game is 'love' used in scoring?"

ANSWER: "Post Office!"

I Never Forget a Face

David Hartman on "Good Morning, America" blooped, "And now Joan People with 'London in the News.' (BREAKING UP) That's Joan London with 'People in the News.' I finally got it out."

Short People

Helen O'Connell was talking with jockey Eddie Arcaro and asked, "Were you always this short?"

He's from Missouri

MAN ON THE STREET: "Here we are at the RCA Exhibition Hall in Radio City, New York. This is an important week in television. We are going to ask the man on the street his opinion of color television. Sir, have you seen color television?"

ANSWER: "Yes, I saw the demonstration ... I won't believe color television until I see it in black and white!"

About Face

MOVIE PREVIEW: "There is sure a gala crowd here tonight at the opening of this great new picture. It seems that half of Hollywood is in New York at the Roxy Theatre for this important opening .... Just about everyone is in white tie and tails. And here is another familiar face coming toward our microphone. Good evening! Would you mind saying a few words to our audience, Miss ... a ... uh ... uh ... I never remember a name, but I always forget a face!"

Does Your Cigarette Taste Different Lately?

COMMERCIAL: "So, friends, when it is time to light up, you will enjoy the freshness and the delicious taste of this mentholated cigarette . . . . Nowhere will you find a bitter-tasting sack of pigarettes!

Test-tickle

On a Seattle student-biology-test broadcast, a junior high school student described an octopus as "an eight-testical monster sometimes found limp on the Washington beaches."

Overkill

Norman Roseman of Brookville Records, who coordinates TV mail orders for *Blooper* record albums, reports about the Englishman doing the color coverage at the Cosmos soccer championship over WNEW in New York. The British commentator blooped, "If the game ends in a tie, there will be sudden over death."

What a Drip

Announcer Doug Weikle on a Minneapolis radio station, doing a commercial for a local loan company, said, "You may need a loan for home repairs, perhaps. Take a leak on your roof, for instance . . ."

Tit for Tat

The announcer on "Hollywood Squares" was listing the prizes when a tight fitting T-shirt was shown on a girl. He blooped, "You can also win this T-shirt by Titto . . . oops, DITTO!"

Silly Ass

NEWSCASTER: "President Carter will meet Anwar Sadat in his upper Ass ... (TURNS PAGE) ... that is, the Aswan Dam in upper Egypt."

Love ... at First Sight

SPORTSCASTER: "We are now getting ready to go into the twelve-point tiebreaker in this exciting tennis match. Borg is ready to serve and is showing Connors his balls."

A Ding-a-Ling

ANNOUNCER: "It's Anaheim, and we are at the Barnum Both-ers, Barnum Brothers, Ringling Brothers Circus ... now wait a minute, let's read it right ... Ringling Brothers ... Here we are at Anaheim at the opening night of Ringling Brothers Branum Braily ... can we do that once more? This is Bob Welles, ladies and gentlemen, the ringmaster for the Branum Bothers Bingling Circus."

I'll Have a Corned Beef on Rye!

DISC JOCKEY: "We hear now theme music from Paramount's new picture starring Frank Sinatra, titled *Papa's Delicatessen* ... uh, that should be *Papa's Delicate Condition*, of course!"

Booze Is the Only Answer

LOCAL NEWSCASTER: "The committee for the charity bazaar starting next Sunday at the Methodist Church has assured us that there will be plenty of booze sold ... I don't mean booze ... I mean that there will be plenty of booths sold!"

He Flipped

Heard on "All My Children": "If your father were alive, he'd turn over in his grave."

Miss Congeniality

INTERVIEWER: "Here we are at the corner of Broad and Fifth Streets interviewing people in and around our great city. Here's a lady coming up to our microphone now. Would you mind telling us your name and what you do for a living?"

LADY: "My name is Myrtle Krause, and I work as a housekeeper for the Van Tillsdale family in Oak Ridge."

INTERVIEWER: "Do you enjoy your work?"

LADY: "Oh, yes. I like my work because the entire family is very congenital to me!"

Plop Plop ... Fizz Fizz

On an Arthur Godfrey program, time was running short. Therefore, two commercials were thrown together back to back. This was the dialogue that resulted from the rushed commercials: "Lipton Soup is what you want for dinner tonight." (NEXT COMMERCIAL) "Thank goodness I brought an Alka-Seltzer!"

Little Boy Lost

An announcer, broadcasting a Pittsburgh Pirates baseball game on radio, described a pop fly that was hit in the direction of the Pirates' five-foot-five shortstop, Clem Kosherek. As the little infielder disappeared from view behind third base, the sportscaster came out with, "Where the hell did Kosherek go?"

Double Trouble

COMMERCIAL: "It's double-feature week ... starting Thursday for four days only, see Bette Davis in *The Virgin Queen* and *Tonight's the Night* ... starting next Monday, be sure to see *Breakthrough* and *Emergency Wedding!*"

When You're Hot ... You're Hot

SPORTSCASTER: "The Bucks, of course, have the nineteen-point lead. They did put the ball up twenty-four times and hit on just one third of those. But the Pistons got hot and shit ... hit on better than fifty-three percent on fourteen out of twenty-six."

On Target

DISC JOCKEY: "Our musical show continues with a medley. We will now hear 'I'm Walking Behind You,' 'Finger of Suspicion,' and 'The Call of the Wild Goose.'"

Screwy

COMMENTATOR: "The auditorium was jam-packed with thousands of constituents who had traveled hundreds of miles to hear the candidate who was seeking reelection. However, public address equipment difficulties were the source of disappointment for the throng, who left without hearing the speaker. It was later learned that the speaker had a screw loose somewhere."

False Alarm

Here is a case where a toothpaste commercial had an untimely "cut in" by a cleansing product. "So, remember, use Pepsodent toothpaste, and brush your teeth . . ." (CUT IN) ". . . right down the drain!"

Stretch Runner

In the heat of the action, sportscasters sometimes get carried away with some weird, picturesque language, as in this classic description during the play-by-play of a nationwide football game on TV.
"Look at him run! He's twisting and squirming like a gal with a flea under her girdle!"

Picked a Pecker

STATION BREAK: "Stay tuned for 'Woody's Pecker Show' . . . 'Woody's Woodpecker Show'!"

Just Heard You on My Toaster

ANNOUNCER: "This is Radio Memphis, WMPS, your Plough, Inc., station, heard on more radios than any other appliances."

In Drag

Milton Cross, veteran announcer best known for his commentary on the Metropolitan Opera, came out with this interesting description of an opening night at the Met. "And the famous Golden Horseshoe is completely filled with beautifully gowned women and formally dressed men with their sparkling necklaces and glittering tiaras."

Fingered

NEWSCASTER: "And the murderer just hung by his fingerprints on the windowsill until the police and fire departments arrived with their outstretched nuts ... I mean, nets!"

Try a Cold Shower

SPORTSCASTER: "Well, they'll sit out their penalty in the dressing room and get a jump on the other guys getting into the shower."

How Dry I Am

SPORTSCASTER: "Good evening, this is Bill Stern. Tonight's story in a moment. If you suffer from dry skin, you will find welcome relief in a Sardo bath. Just one capful of Sardo in your tub bathes away your skin ... I mean ... Dry Skin!"

Bombed

Newsmen who originate their broadcasts from the battlefield are very often frustrated by the sounds of battle, which interfere with their audio report.

NEWSCASTER: "The cavalry's new operation area is very sparsely populated by Vietnamese civilians and heavily infiltrated by North Vietnamese. It's the type of situation that allows the cavalry to bring their full fighting powers ... (BOMB EXPLODES) ... goddamn son of a bitch!"

Stuck in Fly Paper

Former President Gerald Ford, obviously tired after a long, arduous campaign for election, said, "Jimmy Carter talks softly and carries a swy flotter ... a fly flotter ... FLY SWATTER."

No Money Down

On "Bride and Groom" the bride was telling the emcee that she and her new husband were furnishing their home on time payments. The emcee asked if her home was being furnished in a traditional or colonial period. "Oh, no," she replied, "it's being furnished in temporary!"

Hoof and Mouth Disease

Bess Myerson, famous beauty and TV personality, was narrating a TV fashion show. She was describing the fashion models' clothing from head to foot. When she came to one model's shoes, she described them in this way: "Our next model is shoed with the latest high hells ... I mean, is wearing high hell ... well, sometimes they may feel like hell ... but what I meant to say is high heels!!"

Heaven Can Wait

On the audience participation program "Whiz Quiz," emcee Johnny Olsen asked a contestant to finish the following for a valuable prize. "Marriages are made in ____?" The studio audience rocked with laughter as the contestant thought for a moment and answered, "Cleveland?"

What's Cookin'?

STATION PROMOTION: "Stay tuned for another exciting episode of 'The Fugitive,' and see how an innocent man escapes from a bloodthirsty, hungry lunch mob . . . lynch mob!"

Got the World on a String

An announcer doing a commercial for an airline that offered a bargain-priced trip to Hawaii, played a recording of a Hawaiian guitar as background music. He said, "Yes, you can fly to Hawaii for less than you think . . . yes, you can bet your G-string . . . er . . . your G-string on a guitar, that is!!"

Horse Laugh

The following was heard on a Public Service TV special: "As a member of the meat-packing industry, I want to protest the poor timing of the teamsters' union strike just before the holidays. The public is entitled to more consideration and should receive meat for their holiday tables. I want to go on record as saying that I will do everything humanly possible and will not spare the horses to see that meat reaches the public!!"

Leave the Driving to Us

ANNOUNCER: "That's the Wilcox Drive-In . . . on Highway 23 . . . and if you don't know where it is located . . . and most people don't . . . that is to say . . . not too many people know exactly where it is located . . . it is so out of the way . . . I mean, it's right on the highway . . . that is, next to the highway . . . oh, nuts . . . just give me a call, and I'll take you out there!"

You Light Up My Life

NEWSCASTER: "What do you say about Roosevelt that hasn't been said already? He was a legend practically in his own time. The New Deal, the Supreme Court, the jaunty way that he held his cigarette lighter in his mouth. . . ."

Room and Board

Joe Bonomo, former movie actor/strong man, was being interviewed on a radio program. The interviewer asked him whether he had any advice for those suffering with bad backs. He replied, "I very often come up with a sore back as a result of all of the lifting I do. I always get relief by putting a broad under my mattress!!!"

Ready for a Padded Cell

A TV audience was surprised to see a male doing a bra commercial. "Try this wonderful new bra ... you'll especially love the softly lined cups that are so comfortable to wear. You gals who need a little something extra should try model 718. It's lightly padded, and I'm sure you'll love it. I do! ... I mean I like the looks of it ... well ... what I am trying to say is that I don't need one myself naturally, as a man ... but if you do, I recommend it ... How do I know? ... I really don't ... I'm just reading the commercial for Mary Patterson who is ill at home with a cold!"

When He Could Get One

"On Juvenile Jury," popular moppet TV program, host Jack Barry asked a youngster, "Who did the Egyptian princess choose to care for Moses when he was found?" The youngster snapped back, "A baby-sitter!"

Seeing Is Believing

Here is an odd type of Blooper. A TV western series needed some outside location shots to complete one of its episodes. The crew set up its equipment just outside of Newark, New Jersey, and one of the props used as a sign read, "LAST GAS STATION BE-

FORE THE BORDER—TWENTY MILES OF UNIN-
HABITED DESERT AHEAD." Jersey motorists, who
apparently believe in signs, took no chances and lined up at the
prop gas station.

He Blue It!

On the Col. Stoopnagle "Stump Club" quiz program, a contestant was asked, "What does a bride need besides something old,
something new, something borrowed?" The male contestant
snapped back, "A groom!"

Time to Re-tire

ANNOUNCER: "Tonight's program was brought to you by the
McCreary Tire and Rubber Company, maker of fine tires and
rubbers since 1918 . . . I mean rubber tires!"

Order, Please

"Big" Wilson, WIOD, Miami, radio disc jockey and personality,
came out with the following: "So all you do when you are on
your way home is stop by Sears and leave your odor . . .
ORDER!!"

Finger of Suspicion

NEWSCASTER: "Several witnesses at the disaster scene reported that they saw the huge plane suddenly lunge straight
upward in the air. Later, investigation officials said that this was
caused by a goose!"

I'm Ready

FASHION COMMENTATOR: "Our next model will show the latest in hostess gowns. It is a two-piece affair, and it serves a double purpose. It can also be worn in the comfort of your bedroom or for entertaining guests ... just remove the top, and you're ready to go!!!"

Wherever He Wants to Go

When working with animals, the unexpected often happens. Ben the Bear was on a show and went through the usual sit ups, handshakes, etc., for crackers. However, Ben became bored with performing and decided to take a walk to look for a place to take a leak, pulling the microphone, table, trainer, everything in his way, with him.

A Hit and a Miss

SPORTSCASTER: "The Brewers beat the Angels 1-0. Frank Tanana threw a two-hitter for the losers, but Jim Colborn and Ed Rodriguez combined for the three-shit hutout ... three-hit shutout by the Brewers. That's shit on the Sportsline ... IT on the Sportsline!"

Food for Thought

NEWSCASTER: "Winston Churchill has celebrated his eighty-fourth birthday. He ate a thirty-pound birthday cake along with his children and grandchildren."

A Bubu

NEWSCASTER: "Overseas in the Congo this morning all attention is turned toward the United Nations and the appearance of President Kasavubu. But strong man Colonel Joseph Mobutu is himself making a show of force as reported now by ABC correspondent Joseph Kasavubu."

Number One Priority

Here is a classic Blooper from the long-running, popular "Newlywed Game."

EMCEE: "What is the first thing he does before he goes to bed?"

FEMALE CONTESTANT: "We make love, and then we go to sleep. We do it in the bed, but then we go to sleep."

EMCEE: "I think what I should do is perhaps repeat the question. The first thing he does before he goes to bed."

FEMALE CONTESTANT: "To go to sleep?"

EMCEE: "You mean he goes to sleep before he goes to bed?"

FEMALE CONTESTANT: "No, we make love and then go to bed."

EMCEE: "Yeah, I know that."

FEMALE CONTESTANT: "It's a ritual."

EMCEE: "Yeah, yeah, right. It's a heck of a ritual. The first thing he does before he goes to bed."

FEMALE CONTESTANT: "Well, once he gets in bed . . ."

EMCEE: "Well, I don't want to know about that. I want to know BEFORE he gets in bed."

FEMALE CONTESTANT: "He looks at me."

EMCEE: "Thank you. And now to our male contestants . . . what is the first thing you do before you go to bed?"

MALE CONTESTANT: "The first thing that I usually do before I go to bed is urinate!"

Bench Him

NEWSCASTER: "If the full Senate gives its okay, Mrs. Motley will become the first Negro woman to sit on a federal bunch . . . bench!"

A Bad Spell of Weather

WEATHER FORECASTER: "The Weather Bureau radar indicates scattered light snow . . . in the same location as at 5:00 A.M. Therefore, please continue to use the summary that you threw in the wastebasket . . . (BREAKING UP) . . . out of the little round file here. The radar right now shows a scattered broken area of rain showers so a few flowers shit . . . so there are a few showers flitting around. (BREAKING UP) Sioux Falls right now reports light rain showers, uh, light rain showers and sixty-four, Peoria has light drizzle and sixty. (APOLOGIZING) That was a genuine mistake. Fargo, light rain and sixty-eight. Oh, what was I going to say . . . a few showers *flitting* around." (COMPLETE BREAK UP)

Cranky

DISC JOCKEY: "Warner Brothers records would like to take you through . . . (TECHNICAL DIFFICULTIES WITH TURNTABLE) . . . a new album and a turning point for Van Morrison. Okay, man, are you ready to go? C'mon now, crank this motherfucker up!"

A Knockout

One of the great prizefighters of yesteryear, Paulino Uzcudun, had a difficult name to pronounce, as sportscaster Chris Schenkel found out. "The only Basque known in this country was an iron-chinned heavyweight known as Paulino Uz . . . condom . . . who managed to go twelve rounds with Joe Louis."

War of Words

Veteran newsman John Scalli blooped the following: "Colonel Lowell, you pioneered the use of these planes over North Korea at night. What sort of an operation is this?" Lowell replied, "Well, John, it's a new war. It's not North Korea anymore, it's North Vietnam."

Which Hunt

Bob Burns, a popular comedian in the early days of radio, was known for the playing of the bazooka, his own musical creation, and also his sharp wit. He became the innocent victim of a tongue twister when he was a guest on a nationwide radio show.

"I'm going to play a little number that I wrote myself. I'm going to play it on my guitar and sing it to you. It's called the 'Raccoon Cunt' ... ah, the 'Raccoon Hunt.' (AUDIENCE LAUGHTER) I think that you ought to know that they recut these things anyhow. (MORE AUDIENCE LAUGHTER) Oh, you are so nice ... I'm glad that this didn't happen on my show. That certainly would give the Lever Brothers something to fight over. Now I'm going to sing this little number. It's called the 'Raccoon Cunt.' (AUDIENCE HYSTERIA) This is about a time my pa and I went raccoon hunting down in Arkansas."

Viva la France

NEWSCASTER: "A report from France tells of a man who threw everything in his apartment out the second-story window. A big crowd stood around watching—not because of what he was doing, not because of what he was wearing because he was naked, but because he was singing 'The Marseillaise,' and everyone stands around when the French national anthem is played. That's the news, ABC, New York."

That's Rich

The following classic Blooper was made by Senator Barry Goldwater during a speech. "I know of no American who wants to be a rich slave. I know Americans would rather be poor and slaves ... poor and free, I should say."

Georgia On My Mind

A former beauty contest winner, doing her first job as a commentator, blooped, "Well, we have a new Miss America, a Georgia
piece ... peach ... lady from Georgia."

Horse of Another Color

COMMENTATOR: "Nevertheless, this is true. At harness tracks they prevent the appearance of so-called ringers by checking the nuts of the entrants. (BREAKING UP) Chestnuts are the sluggish gray, wart-like formations on the insides of the legs, on all four legs of the horse." (BREAK UP)

Play It Again, Sam

SPORTSCASTER: "Although Sammy Snead is going to have to shoot par golf today if he wants to maintain his lead in the PGA Club Professional Tournament down in Pinehurst, North Carolina, there has to be some unvoiced feelings that Sam doesn't really belong in this tournament since most of the other competitors are legitimate club pros who don't play on the tour. But ole Sam is not one to piss up . . . pass up the opportunity to make an easy buck."

Hard to Swallow

NEWSCASTER: "In Stockholm, doctors have removed a toothbrush from the stomach of a woman. It's been there for sixteen years. How did the toothbrush get into her stomach? Well, the lady says that back in 1952 she had a bad case of stomach upset, and she tried to use a toothbrush to relieve it. She hicced when she should have cupped, and that toothbrush has been in her stomach for sixteen years. (BREAKING UP) That's the news."

The Long and Short of It

Station promos is the term used to describe program advertising. However, promos often become long-winded as in this one for "Long Journey."

ANNOUNCER: " 'Long Journey,' heard every weekday morning on ABC, tells the heartbreak of three lonely people. It's a long journey for Sydney McKenzie, because she's married to Lansing and in love with Wolff. Will Sydney regret her decision to stick by her husband at all costs? She and Lansing have been marooned in Wolff's ranch house by a raging snow storm. Sydney has pneumonia, Lansing a broken arm. Both need care, care that Wolff is willing to give but which Lansing resents because of his seething jealousy of the man who was once married to his wife. But Lansing's jealousy has jumped the bounds of common sense. He struck Wolff in an unreasonable rage. He tried to burn the penicillin intended for Sydney because Wolff was going to administer it. He was striking out at Wolff. Will Lansing destroy what he is trying so desperately to keep, Sydney's love? Hear 'Long Journey' over ABC today. This program came to you from New York. This is the American Broadcasting Company. (OFF MIKE) Who in the hell writes these promos?"

Blackout

NEWSCASTER: "GOP House Leader, Gerald Ford of Michigan, has called for a constitutional amendment to do away with the electrical college ... do away with the electrical col ... electoral college."

Box Lunch

HOST: "Excuse me for a moment while I make contact with Mrs. Louise Jacobs in Detroit, Michigan. Hello, Mrs. Louise Jacobs."

JACOBS: "Hello, there."

HOST: "How are you, Louise?"

JACOBS: "Fine, thank you."

HOST: "Well, I'm happy to hear that, Louise. How's everything in the motor city?"

JACOBS: "Well, everything's all right."

HOST: "Does your husband work in the automobile industy?"

JACOBS: "He's working in a machine shop."

HOST: "He is? Well, what does he do in a machine shop?"

JACOBS: "He's a tool maker."

HOST: "How long have you folks been married?"

JACOBS: "Thirty-two years."

HOST: "Thirty-two years? That's a mighty, mighty long time. Do you have any children?"

JACOBS: "Nine."

HOST: "Your husband's not a tool maker, he's a producer. That's wonderful, wonderful. How did you meet your husband?"

JACOBS: "I met him at the Box Social."

HOST: "At a Box Social? What sort of a Box Social?"

JACOBS: "A Church Box Social."

HOST: "Oh, oh, you mean where everybody brings box lunches and they bid ... that's a real old-fashioned custom. (TRYING NOT TO BREAK UP) The girl brings the box, and the man bids on it, is that the idea?"

JACOBS: "Yes."

HOST: "And how much did he pay for your ... ah ... (AU-DIENCE LAUGHTER) ah ... little package? (AUDIENCE LAUGHTER) You know, I could lose a sponsor for us right now. Well, I bet you had a good time."

Undercover Man

Heard on the TV program "The Nurses": "Due to the fact that silk generates static electricity, it is my duty as a doctor to pay particular attention to the kind of underwear our nurses wear in the operating rooms."

Who's on First

NEWSMAN: "It seems that the majority of the people are confused over Proposition Fourteen. If you are one of those, we advise that you read up on the initiative before going to the polls in November. Remember, if you are for the initiative, you're against the Rumford Fair Housing Bill. If you are against the initiative, you are for the Rumford Fair Housing Bill. We'll try that again. If you are against the initiative ... if you're for the initiative ... you're against ... let's try that again. If you are against the initiative, you're against the ... if you're for the initiative ... if you're for the initiative ... you're against the initiative ..."

Painted into a Corner

NEWSCASTER: "It's 7:16. Drive carefully on your way to work. We have a traffic update coming up in a couple of seconds. Right now, I want to ask you a question. What does Stuart Carey sell? And the third caller who can tell me what Stuart Carey sells will win a gallon of orange label Kotex ... oh, no, can I say that again? You will win a gallon of orange label one-coat *latex* house paint from Stuart Carey."

The Story of His Life

NEWSCASTER: "Writer Clifford Irving entered the Federal Penitentiary at Lewisburg, Pennsylvania, to begin a two-and-a-half-year sentence in the Howard Hughes autobiogarb ... autobiogod ... beograb ... in the autobo ... in a hoax."

A Tale of Two Cities

NEWSCASTER: "You've been listening to the latest news and comment from ABC Radio. Senator Udall says that you can find Naples in New Orleans, the hills of Rome in San Francisco, more Rembrandts in New York than Amsterdam, and more Italian art in the National Gallery in Washington than you will find in any citaly in Italy."

I See

ANNOUNCER: "This message was brought to you by the Upper Midwest Council for better virgins . . . for better vision!"

Udder Hysteria

Cedric Adams was one of early radio's best-known personalities.

ADAMS: "Right now your animal health supplier is giving away free a special introductory-size can of Pfizer Udder Tone. Well, with each twin tube carton of terramycin for mastitis that you buy, you get an introductory-size can of Pfizer Udder Tone. (BREAKING UP) Oh, here we go . . . oh, my goodness. Terramycin, let's get serious, is of course the standard treatment used for . . . (LAUGHING) . . . Listen, I'm going to make it. I've got all day down here. Terramycin is faster, more thorough udder coverage . . . a broad-range treatment can, because of its unique all-liquid formula . . . (LAUGHING) . . . I thought I had it there for a minute. I'm going to make it. I'm halfway through. And you will find Pfizer Udder Tone just great for soothing . . . (MORE BREAKUP) . . . if I give up now, I'll never make it. I've got to face this thing right now or it will be hanging over me all day."

PS: He never made it.

By the Numbers

(TELEPHONE RINGS AND IS PICKED UP.)

FIREMAN: "Fire headquarters in Brooklyn."

NEWS REPORTER: "This is CBS News calling. Is there someone we can speak to for information on the two-alarm fire?"

FIREMAN: "Yes, ma'am. I can give you all the info you want."

NEWS REPORTER: "All right, sir, suppose you give us your name first so that we can identify you."

FIREMAN: "My number is 55."

NEWS REPORTER: "Your name, sir? Can I have your name?"

FIREMAN: "I don't have no name!"

Hot Nuts

NEWSCASTER: "President Carter joined in the singing with Dizzy Gillespie and his jazz musicians during the chorus, singing, 'Salt Peter' . . . (BREAKING UP) 'Salt Peanuts'!"

Oh God-frey

Heard on the Arthur Godfrey morning radio show on CBS: "This is truly a fine product for the relief of aches and pains. So for all of you who find it stiff in the morning, try Bufferin."

Fresh-man

A novice announcer blooped the following: "Tune in tonight at 8:00 P.M. to learn about keeping food fresh. Join Julia Child, the Fresh Chef . . . FRENCH CHEF!"

Tickle Tape

Dick Davis, Miami stock reporter, was the victim of this unexpected interruption:

DAVIS: "At the bell the tickertape shows the Dow Jones Industrial average stood at 983.59, up point 36. Both the transporation and utilities averages showed modest gains ... (TELEPHONE RINGS) ... What? ... Oh, Donna, I'm in the middle of a ... (SLAMS DOWN PHONE) Oh, Christ, damn it, I'm sorry that I have to do this over."

From Hunger

NEWSCASTER: "Vice-president Humphrey got a boost for a new job today. George McGovern, Democrat from South Dakota, says that the vice-president would be a good man to head a worldwide war on Hungary ... er, rather Hunger!"

There's No Place Like Home

LOWELL THOMAS: "Problems up there in space? Oh, yes. Head colds for all three. Also a cabin full of crumbs and water puddles not to mention lack of sleep (BREAKING UP), but everything considered, they report it's still go for a landing." (COMPLETE BREAK UP)

Is This Any Way to Run an Airline?

COMMERCIAL: "So remember ... National Airlines has ten flights daily to Miami and also to Florida."

It Hurts Only when He Laughs

ANNOUNCER: "It's time once again for Paul Harvey and the News."

HARVEY: "Oh, did you see today's *Wall Street Journal,* trying to cheer itself up, reports on a lady who was trying to buy a frilly nightgown for a birthday present for her pet poodle? They didn't have any, but the store clerk said that if you'll measure the dog, we will have one made, and the lady said, 'Oh, I couldn't do that, I want it to be a surprise.'" (BREAK UP)

ANNOUNCER: "One of the most spectacular types of automobile accidents is when the car not only gets banged up, but also bursts into flames. (LAUGHING) What really makes it horrible is the idea that a driver stunned by the accident is trapped inside the burning car. (CONTINUES TO LAUGH) The National Safety Council says that this type of spectacular smashup is very rare. (LAUGHING) ... Good night, Mother ..." (UNABLE TO CONTINUE)

Square Copywriter

COMMERCIAL: "So, ladies, be sure you try the Square Dance Bra. You will find that it holds up beautifully no matter how frantic the fiddling gets!"

Beginner's Luck

Mike Allen, a popular DJ at WLAK, Lakeland, Florida, was recently calling numbers on "Bingo." Somehow he put a number under the wrong letter. In attempting to rectify the confusion, Mike explained, "Folks, you'll have to forgive me today. I've only been married since Sunday, and I don't know which end is which yet! ... I mean which end is up!"

How High Is Up?

On WBZ in Boston the following was heard during the Great Power Failure. A woman, when asked where she had been and what she had been doing when the power failed, replied that she and two hundred others had been stranded on the fifty-second floor of the Prudential tower and that she was "setting up for a cocktail party."

"Did anyone panic?"

"No, they all remained quite calm considering how high they were!"

Back Country

EMCEE: "Our guest speaker on your Rio Grande Valley radio station, who is assisting in promoting McAllen, Texas, as a winter resort and gateway to Mexico, will be Mr. Swollen Rear ... I'm sorry, that should be Mr. Roland Schweer."

Nice Work if You Can Get It

PUBLIC SERVICE ANNOUNCEMENT: "This is your State Employment Service ... attention, women ... quit walking the streets and come to see us for steady employment."

North of the Border

Heard on WOBT, Rhinelander, Wisconsin: "Mexican officials have given approval of the U.S. air search for a missile that went off course and apparently landed in an uninhibited part of northern Mexico."

Time Out

On a Denver radio station a disc jockey told his listeners, "While this record is playing, I had better run out and put some more money in the marking peter, that is ... the parking meter!"

Winchester Cathedral

ANNOUNCER: "A plague was presented to the congregation of St. Peter's Lutheran Church by Mr. and Mrs. Ray Hulver of Winchester ... of course, I mean plaque!"

Join the Foreign Legion

On TV station WCYB, Bristol, Tennessee, a "March of Dimes Telerama" fund-raising campaign was held to aid the victims of polio and birth defects. A well-meaning American Legion Post Commander presented his check with this comment: "The Legionnaires of our post present the $100 check for the March of Dimes ... and we do hereby pledge ourselves to help all we can to further birth defects."

Quick on the Draw

Jim Dunlap, disc jockey for WQAM, Miami, was talking to another DJ. He told him that his shoe was untied, and when the other DJ bent over to tie it, Dunlap cried out, "Watch it, your zippie is open ... I mean, your Zippie chocolate drink with the cap open!"

Sticky Problem

When the winner was crowned Miss North Carolina State, a local mayor was called on to present the attractive young lady with a corsage. As he nervously attempted to pin the small grouping of flowers on the girl's gown, she was heard to say, "Ouch! Mr. Mayor, this gown is strapless!"

Toilet Trained

When Art Linkletter appeared as emcee of "Hollywood Talent Scouts," he interviewed Charlie Weaver. He told Charlie, "You are just like interviewing my five-year-olds; you never know what they are going to squirt! (AUDIENCE LAUGHTER) Now, audience, you know what I mean!"

Whoops

Pee Wee Reese, during a play-by-play telecast between the New York Yankees and the Washington Senators, came up with the following: "Mike McCormick decides he needs another ball and the umpire throws it up . . . I mean, the umpire throws up . . . the umpire throws the ball up!"

Horse and Buggy

COMMERCIAL: ". . . so, remember, for the finest in foods and atmosphere, try your nearby Red Roach Inn . . . I mean, Red Coach Inn!"

Down in the Mouth

On "The Today Show" Hugh Downs told about the dangers of youngsters dropping out of school . . . "which can very often result in illegitimacy . . . I mean illiteracy!"

Strange Bedfellows

Merv Griffin had the Duke and Duchess of Bedford as his guests. The Duke told of the castle in which they lived in England and boasted of having fifty-four rooms. Griffin asked, "What is your favorite room, Your Grace?" The Duke snapped back, "The bedroom!"

Even Your Best Friend Won't Tell You

Miami's sportscaster and former college football coach Tom Nugent told his TV viewers about a Miami Dolphins pro football star: "I'll tell you more about the Dolphins' offensive end after this message from Ban Deodorant!"

Foreigner

On the popular "Newlywed Game" the emcee asked the female contestants, "From what foreign country would your husband buy you a car?" One of the female contestants answered, "Texas!"

Behind the Eight Ball

Network newscaster Don Gardner, announcing the news of eight children being born in South America, blooped, "This was the first recorded octopus birth in history ... that should be octuple!"

Wild, Wild World of Sports

SPORTSCASTER: "... so be sure that you stay tuned to this station where you will see the elimination of the heavyweight fighters after this football game."

Adult Bookstore

POLITICAL BROADCAST: "And the National Committee is planning to assemble all of the Senator's speeches and remarks and put them in a handsome bound book and offer it for sale to the general public, the profits of which will go to the party. A book such as this is certain to be destined for immorality ... er ... immortality!"

Hurry Up and Wait

PUBLIC SERVICE ANNOUNCEMENT: "So when you are lost in the deep woods, don't panic, just drop a postcard to Forest Department, Box 853, Burlington, Vermont, for your free booklet, which covers just such situations."

Beauty and the Beast

Ted Steele, former DJ, was master of ceremonies of the Miss U. S. Television contest, the first of which was won by Edie Adams. Ted gave one of the contestants the following introduction: "Our next finalist is a lovely miss who is going to sing Victor Herbert's 'Ah, Sweet Mystery of Life.' When you see her, I know you will agree that her breath will take your beauty away!"

Havin' a Ball

SPORTSCASTER: "Here we are in the ninth inning of this crucial championship ladies' softball game between the Atlantic Powder Puffs and the Richmond Curlers. The Curlers are three runs behind with all the bags loaded."

Dropouts

Dick Cavett, emcee of his own popular nighttime TV program, was discussing the Miss America Pageant. He quite innocently observed, "I understand that the Miss America Pageant will drop bathing suits for talent appraisal." When the studio audience tittered, he apologized by saying, "Now, that didn't come out right, did it?"

No Bull

Poor timing between live action and commercials can produce some unfortunate results. Such was the case with sportscaster Jimmy Powers. He was describing a rodeo from Madison Square Garden when the radio station took a break from the action in the arena for a commercial. The announcer extolled the virtues of Maxwell House coffee. At the instant the commercial ended, the camera returned to live action where the excited Jimmy shouted, "That's a lot of bull!" as the bull-riding event was already in progress.

Gopher Balls

Sportscaster Wyn Elliot, before the British Open, told his central U. S. A. radio audience, "And now for some gopher profiles of Jack Nicklaus, Tony Jacklin, and Lee Trevino. (LAUGHING) I mean golfer profiles."

X-Rated

ANNOUNCER: "Our late show movie tonight is the rollicking comedy *Boy Mates Girl.* (BREAKING UP) I'm sorry, that should be *Boy Meets Girl!*"

A Dirty Old Man

This slip was heard on "Sale of the Century," an NBC audience-participation program. The emcee said, "Now here is a ten-point question. We know that a man who explores outer space is called an astronaut. What do you call a man who explores underwear? . . . Ooops . . . I mean underwater!"

Fun City

NEWSCASTER: "Here are today's top stories. Arthur Goldberg and Nelson Rockefeller, both candidates for governor of the state of New York, attend fun-raising dinners in New York City as election time nears."

Nuts to You

On an audience-participation program, members from the audience were called on to read the sponsor's commercial. A pretty young lady with a deep southern accent was asked to read the blurb for Planters peanuts, which resulted in, "So, remember, ladies, next time you are out shopping, be sure to ask your grocer for southern-planted roasted penis."

Screwball

"Double or Nothing" was one of early-day radio's most popular quiz shows. It was emceed by Walter O'Keefe, who was the victim of this contestant's unplanned answer on his live radio show.

O'KEEFE: "I'd rather see you win here today than anybody else up here."

CONTESTANT: "I'd like to."

O'KEEFE: "You're not married?"

CONTESTANT: "No."

O'KEEFE: "Anna, tell me, have you had any unusual experiences in your work as a waitress?"

CONTESTANT: "Oh, yes, there were several."

O'KEEFE: "For instance, anything that we could do with a daytime audience . . . you know what I mean?"

CONTESTANT: "Oh, sure. Yesterday ... I'd hate to embarrass the man ... but he asked me a question that I didn't know how to answer. He told me about a friend who went to the doctor, and he was very sick, and they didn't know what to do with him. I asked him what the trouble was. He said that he couldn't go out nights, can't eat. He can't do nothing. He said that he sent his wife away on a vacation, so what do you think we should do with him. I said, well, I don't know, what's your suggestion. Well, he said, I think that he should get a good-looking girl like you and take her home, and just have a big screwing party ..."

O'KEEFE: "Now, Anna, why ..."

CONTESTANT: "I told him that he should go down to a hardware store and get a screw ..."

O'KEEFE: "Anna, why don't we just go on with the questions that we have!"

Making Waves

DISC JOCKEY: "... and now, rock 'n' rollers, the next platter is dedicated to all you surfers. So let's all grab our broads and ride ... ride ... ride!"

From the Chandelier

Veteran Kansas broadcaster Charley Whitworth reports that one particularly hectic night at one of the Wichita TV stations, a new, young announcer committed this gem. The garage door special from the Overhead Door Company proved too much as the young fellow earnestly declared, "This special on home-type garage doors ends Saturday at 5:00 P.M. at the Overdead Whore Company."

Dog Gone It

ANNOUNCER: "Tune in Sunday evening at 7:30 for a treat for the entire family, especially the children. Walt Disney's *One Hundred and one Damnations* . . . I mean *DALMATIONS!*"

Fall Classic

SPORTSCASTER: "Penn squeaked by Army twenty-one to twenty, Michigan overwhelmed Northwestern thirty-four to seven, North Carolina tripped LSD . . . LSU!"

Sour Grapes

STATION PROMOTION: "Stay tuned for one of the all-time film classics, John Steinbeck's *Rapes of Grath.*"

Blow Up

Merv Griffin had a nine-year-old stock investor, Stanley Martinez, as a guest. Apparently nervous, he let out a large burp. The youngster ad libbed, "I know I have some oil, but not gas." Merv replied, "I know your gas must be natural."

Burned Up

DISC JOCKEY: "This is WPOP radio in Hartford, Connecticut . . . ah, shit, I just stuck my elbow in the ashtray and burned a fifteen-dollar shirt, let alone my pink little bod."

Talk, Talk, Talk

Newscaster Frank McGee, reporting the latest vote count on NBC-TV's "Election Seventy," announced that Governor Davis of Vermont had won reelection. "It is believed that his fine work in the area of pollution and conversation was largely responsible."

A Horse's Ass

This incident occurred years ago on "The Marshal of Gunsight Pass," a live show, which was seen on KECA-TV (now KABC-TV). In one episode duly recorded by the television camera, the intrepid marshal leaped astride his steed and rode off facing the horse's tail.

Jockey Shorts

DISC JOCKEY: "Good afternoon, rock 'n' roll fans, this is your groovy dick jockey, Disk Young, welcoming you to another rock session. Did I say dick jockey? . . . Oh, my God!"

Coffee, Tea, or Milk

Doug Koelemay of KTBS-TV, of Shreveport, Louisiana, was giving his evening newscast. In it was a story about an impending airlines strike. In the course of his report, he said, "The stewardesses and pursuers . . . that is pursers . . . could possibly go on strike tomorrow."

Career Highlight

NEWSCASTER: "Speaker of the House McCormack has been investigated for alleged irregular lobbying practices. Speaker of the House is a high office, and Mr. McCormack is about as high as you can get."

Temper, Temper

STATION BREAK: "Stay tuned for the Ingrid Bergman Festival, *Winter Light,* starring Ingmar Bergman ... that should be Ingrid Thulen in the Ingrid Bergman Festival ... that should be Ingmar Bergman Festival starring Ingrid ... (IN EXASPERATION) ... Tune in at 8:30 and see for yourself!"

Night Kapp

The following Blooper was heard on radio station KAPP, Redondo Beach, California: "That was Sinatra ... and the time on the Krap chonometer is midnight ... I'm sorry, that should have been the Kapp chronometer."

Royal Flush

NEWS DOCUMENTARY: "This is Les Smith, WIOD News. Twenty-five years ago on April 28, 1945, the body of Benito Mussolini was hung by the heels at a Milan, Italy, filling station. Mussolini had proclaimed himself the Douche, the new leader. He promised a new Roman Umpire ... that should be Il Duce."

Dishpan Hands

Robert Goulet starred in his own TV series "Blue Light." One scene showed a German guard on duty. The guard was in the process of lighting a cigarette when an arm came from behind him and grabbed him. However, when the arm appeared, the sound of the commercial advertising a dish detergent cut in with, "Would you believe these are the hands of a grandmother?"

College Try

Heard on the National Educational Television network: "All female students who are interested in going to medical school should first satisfy the dean at the university."

True and False

The following Blooper was heard on a New Westminster, British Columbia, radio station: "Here's Rusty Draper singing 'The Shitting, Whiftering Sands' . . . er, I mean 'The Shiftering, Whistering Sands' . . . boy! . . . You can't trust these store-bought teeth . . . that should be 'Shifting, Whispering Sands' . . . Whew!"

Heads I Win, Tails You Lose

When I was a guest of Larry King, WIOD, Miami, radio personality who is heard on the Mutual Network, he told me about a stumbling block preceding each Miami Dolphins football game for which he did the color commentary. "Well, it's that time again. The referees and team captains are on the fifty-yard line for the turn coss."

A Gasser

Jim Lang, emcee of TV's popular "Dating Game," introduced a Miss Cynthia Wilson. He enthusiastically described her as the Hollywood Grass Girl of the Year. (AUDIENCE LAUGHTER) "Of course, I meant Hollywood Gas Girl of the Year, representing the Hollywood Gas Company."

Ladies' Man

SPORTSCASTER: "In lane four is three-time AAU swimming star Fred Hendrix. Fred is expected to easily win this title again as he is rated as the undisputed breast-stroking champion in this event."

Fly Me

NEWSCASTER: "The president and prime minister of India appear to have made progress in their discussions. A pesty fly seemed to be hovering over the president. Trying to be a help, the prime minister wacked the president's fly."

Bleep

ANCHORMAN: "For an obscene report, we call in our roving reporter . . . on-the-scene report!"

Signs of the Times

NEWSCASTER: "Jimmy Carter's drop in popularity has caused some humorous bumper snickers . . . stickers on automobiles."

In like Flynn

STATION PROMO: " 'Baretta' will be in a new slut on Wednesday . . . that should be a new time slot."

Try Peanuts

COMMERCIAL: "So, friends, be sure to visit Frankie's fine restaurant for elephant food and dining ... the portions may be elephant size ... but I meant to say elegant food and dining!"

Small Talk

Sandy Hill on "Good Morning, America," told her audience to be sure to watch "the miseries about camping." (LAUGHING) "Of course, that should be the mini-series about camping."

That's My Pop

NEWSCASTER: "Princess Caroline, daughter of Prince Rainer and Grace Kelly, was given two royal balls by her father prior to her marriage."

Fore-cast

The following was uttered by a weather forecaster who told us that he committed a Freudian slip. He had an important golf date when his weather forecast was finished. He blooped, "The weather appears to be threatening with storms brewing off the golf course . . . I mean, Gold Coast."

That's Where the Action Is

NEWSCASTER: "Washington secretary Elizabeth Ray told newsmen about her many sexual exploits in the Capital City. More action news in a minute."

Think Positive

COMMERCIAL: "So, you women who are thinking about a second car, go to your nearest Volkswagen dealer for a Rabbit test."

The People's Choice

ANNOUNCER: "You can always come to your little home-maker's helper, Howie Rankin, the people's peter pleaser . . . the Peters' people pleaser."

Today . . . No One Would Notice

Sid Caeser tells about a skit in which he participated on his "Show of Shows," produced by Max Liebman. The program was live, and he didn't have enough time to change his costume for the next skit. As a result, in a bus skit that he was doing with Imogene Coca, he appeared in a leopard-skin costume carrying a spear and wearing sandals.

Falsies

NEWSCASTER: "The FTA is cracking down on misleading advertising. The latest to be scrutinized is Poly-Grip for false advertising."

Bare Facts

A woman on a quiz show was asked who Pete Rose is, to which she answered, "Oh, I've heard of him. His name's been in the paper lately. Isn't he some kind of streaker?"

Tim, Dick, and Hurry

Tom Brokaw of the NBC's "Today Show" was rushing to finish the following promo before a station break. "Our next guest will tell of his homosexual experiences with Dick Schapp . . . that isn't exactly what I mean. He will discuss with Dick Schapp his homosexual experiences."

Read All about It

NEWSCASTER: "In Washington, General Bradley's speech today was one of several interesting news developments dealing with our military defenses. Here's a summary by Gunner Back. (SILENCE) We seem to be unable to contact Washington at this time. We'll try it once again. Our cue to Washington is, 'Here is a summary by Gunner Back.' (SILENCE) Sorry, we seem to be unable to, for some inexplicable reason, contact Gunner Back in Washington, even as we have contacted him every night for the past eight years. Now then, to the nation's sports fans, the biggest news in quite awhile is building tonight in Chicago where world heavyweight champion Rocky Marciano is about to meet that challenge by ex-champ Jersey Joe Wolcott. We sent correspondent Tom Casey to the weighing-in ceremonies today, and he recorded this report at that dramatic scene. (SILENCE) Mother told me there would be days like this. We'll try once again for Chicago. Calling Tom Casey in Chicago. Our cue is, 'This report at that dramatic scene.' (SILENCE) Unfortunately, we had been told earlier today that Tom Casey had recorded a very fascinating report at the weighing-in ceremonies, and he had the voices of both Joe Wolcott and Rocky Marciano. Let's see what else we have in the news to talk about this evening on a memorable 'Headline Edition,' at least to me ... suppose we come back to you in just a moment or two. On this cue, I'll be back in a minute with more news."

ANNOUNCER: " 'Headline Edition' is one of over sixty ABC news shows brought to you each week by a distinguished staff of reporters, analysts, and commentators. ABC specializes in swift, accurate, and complete reporting of the latest happenings here and abroad. That kind of news coverage just doesn't happen. (BREAKING UP) A trained newsman fills in the coloring, bringing the events to life, but it takes an experienced ... (LAUGHING) ... correspondent to know how that event fits the overall news pattern. Now here again is 'Headline Edition' with portions transcribed, what portions, that's 'Headline Edition.' "

Miss-take

When I appeared as a guest with Tom Snyder, Tom was telling viewers about Ruth Gordon, who also appeared as a guest. "Our guest will be the distinguished actress Ruth Gordon, following this commercial. Don't fail to miss it."

Oy Vey!

ANNOUNCER: "Tonight's 'Sermonette' features Rabbi Irving Mosckowitz of the Temple Emanuel Reform School ... I beg your pardon, that should be Reform Shul."

You Really Know How to Hurt a Guy

Panelists very often evoke some unpredictable Bloopers due to the unplanned questions and answers. One such moment occurred when I appeared as a guest on the Goodson-Todman produced "To Tell the Truth." Panelist Peggy Cass asked me, "Did our host, Mr. Moore, ever do anything naughty on the air ... and is it true that he once did a dance with not all of his clothes buttoned up by mistake? Would that be considered a Blooper since it was a visual joke?"

MOORE (INDIGNANTLY): "A visual joke? I must say I have been injured deeply in my time, but I am wounded to the quick, and I have a very slow quick!" Needless to say, the audience howled at this double entendre.

Turned On

The following was heard on the Public Broadcasting network: "We are now going to show you how the sperm creates life, which should be of great interest to you students. This demonstration is stimulated ... I mean simulated."

When You Fly ... Be Sure to Take a Plane

In 1956 American Forces Network newsman Chuck Roberts was meeting Australian Prime Minister Robert Menzies in Frankfurt, Germany, at the Rhine-Main Airport. Menzies had been traveling for twenty-six hours and was obviously tired.

ROBERTS: "Mr. Menzies, what brings you to Germany?"

MENZIES: "An airplane!"

I'll Drink to That

Heard over a local newscast on station WJOY, Burlington, Vermont, during the pre-Christmas season, 1969: "Roger Sheridan, State Liquor Commissioner, says that Vermont can look forward to a joyful season. The state liquor whorehouse is filled to capacity!"

A Great Finish

At WFIL, Philadelphia, newscaster Bob Johnson finished his fifteen-minute newscast. A visitor in the studio, thinking the microphone was off, said, "Best goddamn newscast I ever heard you do, Bob." "Oh, bullshit," Bob answered. He freely admits that he never worked at the station again.

Can't See the Forest for the Trees

A talk show hostess at a Los Angeles television station introduced the star of the highly successful "F Troop" television show as follows: "Our guest today is the sergeant of that wonderfully funny TV series 'F Troop.' Let's hear a warm welcome for Torrest Fucker! ... well ... ah ... a little joke there. Oh, my God!"

On the Pot

Newsman Frank Lynn, WPLG, Miami, after a major marijuana bust, told viewers, "It appears to be the largest pot hole in Florida history . . . I mean, pot haul."

Sweater Girl

On "Hollywood Squares," host Peter Marshall asked a female contestant, "If you feel drowsy at the wheel of a car, you should take off something, what?" She answered, "Your sweater . . . no, I'm only teasing you." Marshall replied, "Everytime you take off your sweater, you tease me!"

Equal Rights

Radio and TV personality Virginia Graham is the victim of uncontrollable laughter when something strikes her funny when she's on the air.

ANNOUNCER: "And now Virginia Graham answers her mail."

GRAHAM: "Today's letter is from Mrs. C. S. And Mrs. C. S. has a problem with her husband. He hasn't been coming home at night and giving her the marital devotion that she feels is necessary. She has lived with him for several years, and she feels that this is an indication of perhaps a sterility or a desire to have . . . (UNCONTROLLABLE LAUGHTER) . . . I'm not supposed to do this on the air, and I've promised that I wouldn't do it anymore . . ."

ANNOUNCER: "Virginia, dear, I'll take care of it. (GRAHAM STILL LAUGHING IN BACKGROUND.) We'd better take a cutaway now, and then we will come back again in just a moment."

This concludes . . . this conclees . . . that is all!!!